on

Long Island

ALICE M. GEFFEN

&

CAROLE BERGLIE

Backcountry Publications
Woodstock, Vermont

An invitation to the reader

If you find that conditions have changed along these walks, please let the authors and publisher know so that corrections may be made in future printings. Address all correspondence to:

Editor, Walks and Rambles™ Series
Backcountry Publications
PO Box 748
Woodstock, Vermont 05091

Library of Congress Cataloging-in-Publication Data
Geffen, Alice M.
    Walks and rambles on Long Island / Alice M. Geffen and
Carole Berglie.
        p. cm.
    Includes bibliographical references and index.
    ISBN 0-88150-339-8 (alk. paper)
    1. Walking—New York (State)—Long Island—Guidebooks.
    2. Hiking—Guidebooks. 3. Long Island (N.Y.)—Guidebooks.
    I. Berglie, Carole. II. Title.
GV199.42.N652L664   1996
917.47'21—dc20   95-52150
                                                                CIP

Poems by May Swenson used with permission of the Literary Estate of May Swenson.

Published by Backcountry Publications
A division of The Countryman Press
PO Box 748
Woodstock, VT 05091

Distributed by W.W. Norton & Company, Inc.
500 Fifth Avenue
New York, NY 10110

Printed in the United States of America

Book design by Sally Sherman
Maps by Alex Wallach, © 1996 The Countryman Press
Cover photo of Clifftop Trail, Montauk Bluffs by Diane Gorodnitzki
All interior photographs by the authors, unless otherwise credited

In memory of Michael Psareas,
naturalist, scholar, friend

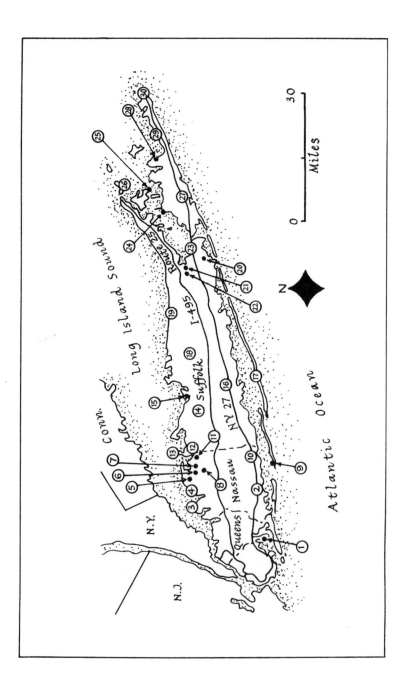

Contents

Preface

"You come from Loooonng Island," the man said as he filled the gas tank of our van. We were in Wyoming, about as far away from Long Island as we cared to be. Hey, Wyoming's a great place, but what do people do there when they want an ocean view?

Long Island enjoys a peculiar fame. Its proximity to Manhattan makes it the stepchild of a hectic, cosmopolitan region. People elsewhere in the country see it as split-level houses and Dashing Dans, as a land of shopping malls and superconsumers. Even people as close as New York City think there's little more here than an expressway to the Hamptons. But as anyone who lives on Long Island knows, there's a lot more going on. Part suburbs, part city, part country—the island is big enough to encompass it all.

We've been fortunate in that, although there has been considerable development on Long Island, there have also been meaningful attempts to save habitat. We have a national seashore and several national wildlife refuges, state parks and preserves, county parks, township properties, Nature Conservancy lands, and private areas open to the public. Rather than mourn what has been lost, this book celebrates what remains.

Walks and Rambles on Long Island describes thirty natural areas open to the public. The walks are short—most are about a mile—and easy to navigate, with good trail markers and cleared paths. Some areas are accessible to people in wheelchairs, and if that's the case, we've noted it at the end of the "Access" section. If a permit is required for entry, or there is a fee, we've noted that, too.

The book is divided into three sections: Queens and Nassau, Western and Central Suffolk, and Eastern Suffolk—including the East End. Within each section, the walks are arranged geographically from west to east.

Be a responsible visitor. Obey the rules at each preserve and stay on the trail. Also, be considerate of others who might be outdoors enjoying a walk through the woods. Move slowly, and look around you. Listen to bird songs, smell the flowers. We've described some of what you're likely to see at each preserve, but that's just to get you started. If you like, carry a field guide with you so you can identify new birds or plants. Binoculars make it easier to distinguish the field marks of birds; a hand lens is helpful for examining wildflowers. Consider bringing your children on some of the trails, but be sure they understand that seeing animals and enjoying nature require being quiet.

Caution: As you're no doubt aware, ticks that carry disease do occur in some areas of Long Island. Ticks can be found in any outdoor location with vegetation, even a back yard, but the more likely spots are high grass, dense shrubbery, and salt marshes. Ticks get on you if you brush up against them. Then they usually walk around for a while before attaching themselves to you, and only then do they bite you and begin to feed. A tick bite does not cause disease unless the tick is infected. Additionally, it takes as long as forty-eight hours for an infected tick to transmit Lyme disease after biting you.

You should not curtail your enjoyment of the outdoors, but you should be tick-aware. Educate yourself about the two kinds of ticks we have on Long Island: the tiny deer tick and the larger dog tick. When you are taking a trail, follow these precautions:

1. Wear light-colored clothes so you can easily spot a tick on you. Wear long pants and tuck them into your socks or boots. Do not go barefoot or in sandals (never a smart thing to do in the woods, anyway).
2. For extra protection, spray your shoes and clothing with insect repellent—if possible, one containing up to 30 percent DEET. Check the label and use as directed; some sprays should not be used on bare skin.
3. Walk in the center of woodland trails to avoid brushing against vegetation. Check yourself routinely for "hitchhikers."
4. When you return home, check your clothing again and put it in the laundry. Examine your body for ticks, and if possible take a shower. Check the interior of your car; we find that ticks often slip off us and take up residence in the car for a few days after a walk.

5. If you should find a tick attached to your skin, promptly, gently, and firmly remove it, preferably with a fine-tipped tweezers. Do not use your bare fingers, and do not squeeze the tick. Also, do not apply mineral oil or Vaseline to remove the tick. Pull with the tweezers as close to the mouth (of the tick) as possible and firmly tug. Don't twist. Then apply an antiseptic to the site.

6. Save the tick and label it with the date, where it was on your body, and where you picked it up. Watch to see if a rash develops—not necessarily at the bite; if so, contact your doctor promptly.

Scientists are testing a vaccine for Lyme disease; it may be available by 1997.

Acknowledgments

We would like to thank Sara Davison, executive director of The Nature Conservancy on Long Island, for her continuing support and enthusiasm for this book. The Nature Conservancy's active program of acquisition and preservation ensures the continuance of nature conservation on Long Island.

Thanks are also due to the many park rangers, wildlife biologists, and other park employees who provided information, and to our fellow walkers—Andrew Rubenfeld, Janet Robertson, and Zan Knudson.

Introduction

In many parts of the world, a major geographical feature such as a mountain range defines the character of the land. Long Island has no mountains. For us, the major geographical feature is the water that surrounds us—the Atlantic Ocean to the south and east, Long Island Sound to the north, and the East River to the west. Nassau and Suffolk Counties alone have 1,180 miles of shoreline. For Long Island especially, it is the steady and ceaseless action of ocean waves and currents that shapes and reshapes the island.

For instance, because of ocean action, sand is carried away from Montauk Point and deposited on Fire Island. Indeed, Fire Island has grown almost five miles to the west since the lighthouse was built in 1858. Waves and currents also produce spits and sandbars, while the tides twice daily replenish our brackish lagoons and estuaries.

A Glacial Heritage

Underlying Long Island is the same Jurassic-era bedrock upon which Manhattan's skyscrapers are built. It is topped with a thick deposit of sands, clays, and gravels that was laid down during the Cretaceous period, about 80 million years ago. But there is little evidence of these rocks and deposits on Long Island today. Instead, our present landscape is marked by the changes that the last continental glacier made when it began to retreat a mere 50,000 years ago.

During the Pleistocene epoch, this final (we hope) mass of ice reached its most southerly point somewhere in the middle of Long Island. As the climate warmed and the ice retreated, about 15,000 years ago, the glacier left a terminal moraine—a large ridge of rocks and boulders. Referred to as the Ronkonkoma moraine, it forms the backbone of Long Island and stretches from northern Queens all the way out to Montauk.

South of the terminal moraine lies what is called the outwash plain—an area of flat, sandy soil dissected by small streams. Basically, this is the southern coast of Long Island. North of the Ronkonkoma

A woodland scene

moraine is another ridge, running roughly from Lake Success out along the North Fork. This has been termed the Harbor Hill moraine, a second ridge formed by the glacier as it paused in its retreat to Canada. And between the two ridges is the only river on Long Island that flows from west to east—the Peconic River.

As the glacier retreated, it left large boulders scattered about, as well as big chunks of ice. The boulders are still here, and are called erratics; they are easy to spot along North Shore beaches. The large chunks of ice melted and made ponds, called kettle holes; most of the lovely woodland ponds on the North Shore are kettle holes. The immense quantities of water produced by the melting glacier caused the oceans to rise to the level we know now—over 350 feet higher—flooding lower areas and giving Long Island its characteristic fish shape.

We mention all this because these defining features are what give Long Island's wild areas their uniqueness. The type of soil and terrain, the ponds and streams, the boulders and sea cliffs are host to our particular plants and animals. They are the features you'll see as you walk the trails described in this book.

Our Native Plants

As the glacier retreated, the newly exposed earth was colonized by lichens and then other plants that like cold weather, such as hemlocks. But as the climate warmed up more, some of those cold-weather plants died and trees and plants that favor temperate conditions began to grow here. And this process seems to be continuing. Long Island is largely a buffer zone between two major vegetative zones: the Canadian to the north and the Carolinean to the south. As most gardeners know, we're fortunate enough to be able to grow both some of these northern species and many of the southern ones in our gardens.

So when you're on the trails of the North Shore, notice the rocky, heavy, and rich soil and the lush mix of hemlock, sweetgum, tulip tree, yellow birch, spicebush, arrowwood, and white oak. Woodlands dotted with freshwater ponds and streams are home to wildflowers such as Canada mayflower, Solomon's seal and false Solomon's seal, jack-in-the-pulpit, forget-me-not, and pickerelweed, as well as a variety of ferns and mosses.

Along the South Shore, the soil is sandier and the vegetation is sparser; oaks, hickories, and pines predominate. Elsewhere, the salt marshes and bays are areas of thick, supersaturated mud and mats of cordgrass and phragmites. These wetlands are gradually filling in with sediment and vegetation, protected from destructive wave action by long barrier beaches. And beaches present their own, very different vegetative environment. Beach goldenrod, pearly everlasting, glasswort, marsh mallow, sea lavender, and beach plum are familiar sights. The beach grasses, so graceful in the coastal breezes, have strong roots that help anchor the dunes.

Certainly a most notable feature of Long Island vegetation is its pine barrens. With over 18 million acres of forested land, New York State has had but two state forest preserves, one in the Adirondacks and one in the Catskills. Now there is a third: the Long Island Pine Barrens. The impetus for preserving the last remaining expanse of undeveloped land on Long Island was water; it was the only way to ensure an adequate supply of drinking water for the 2.6 million residents of Nassau and Suffolk Counties. In the bargain, more than 53,000 acres of ecologically rare habitat are spared the chain saw and bulldozer, and an additional 47,000 acres of buffer zone will be developed, but only under strict controls.

The beauty and wealth of the pine barrens are subtle. Early settlers viewed the area as "barren." An 1860 gazetteer of New York State describes the land as "almost sterile plains or barren sandhills . . . occupied by 'brush plains' which are sparsely inhabited and hardly susceptible of cultivation." A footnote regarding the burning over of the land in 1844 and 1845 notes "these lands are valuable only for the timber upon them; and when that is destroyed they become nearly worthless." Yet here you'll find rare and unusual species of wildflowers such as the rose coreopsis and the fibrous bladderwort.

The Animals

We no longer have many large native mammals on Long Island, but there still are abundant deer, foxes, raccoons, muskrats, rabbits, opossum, squirrels, and chipmunks as well as mice, shrews, and moles. Salamanders, turtles and tortoises, frogs, and a few nonpoisonous snakes also find home here.

Long Island is renowned for its birds. Indeed, well over 350 species have been seen (not counting accidentals or strays), of which about 150 species are nesters. In winter, after many of our nesting birds have moved southward, the island is host to a variety of northern birds, many of which reach their southern limit here: great cormorants, harlequin ducks, king and common eiders, Iceland gulls, razorbills, snowy owls, crossbills, and redpolls. Each spring and fall, a massive migration of shorebirds and songbirds passes through Long Island, largely concentrated in the western end. And throughout the spring and summer, our many nesting and resident birds fill the air with song.

These are some of the basic elements that constitute Long Island's natural resources. In spite of all our highways and people, there's still a lot of unspoiled land. But remember that nature is always changing. Wind and wave action reshape our coastline; big storms bring down tall trees and give understory plants a chance to grow; and warmer winters allow more birds to remain year-round. It is our hope that the walks in this book will show you some of these processes, and grant you heightened understanding of the natural world in which you live.

Queens and Nassau

Butterflyweed

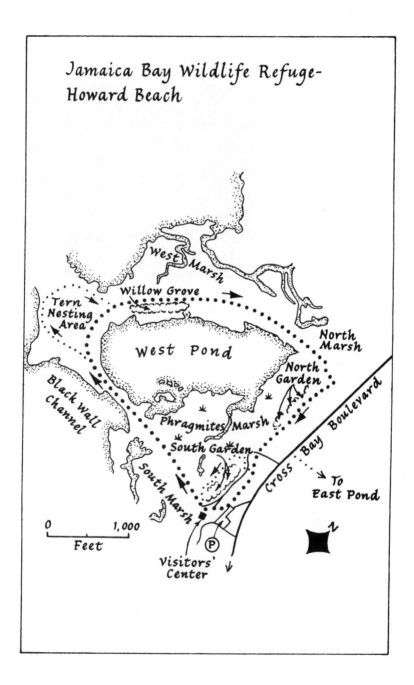

Jamaica Bay Wildlife Refuge-
Howard Beach

West Marsh

Willow Grove

Tern
Nesting
Area

West Pond

North
Marsh

North
Garden

Black
Wall
Channel

Phragmites Marsh

South Garden

Cross Bay Boulevard

To
East Pond

South Marsh

0   1,000
    Feet

P

Visitors'
Center

Jamaica Bay
Wildlife Refuge

Location: Cross Bay Boulevard, Howard Beach, Queens
Owner: National Park Service
Distance: 1½ miles

Jamaica Bay is a unit of Gateway National Recreation Area, a vast, federally owned and managed area that includes Jacob Riis Park and Floyd Bennett Field, both in Brooklyn; Great Kills Park in Staten Island; and Sandy Hook in northeastern New Jersey. Together, the units add up to 26,000 acres of wooded uplands, ocean beaches, dunes, and bays. The Jamaica Bay Unit includes Floyd Bennett Field, New York's first municipal airport. But it is the wildlife refuge that interests us here.

Known worldwide as a birding hotspot, Jamaica Bay's bird list is well over 300 species. In fact, we've seen over 100 on a single spring day! Birders are also getting into butterflies these days, and the refuge has recently put up boxes and planted shrubs to attract butterflies. Checklists of both birds and butterflies are available at the visitors' center.

Access

From the Southern State (or Belt) Parkway, take exit 17S. Go south on Cross Bay Boulevard through the town of Howard Beach. Proceed 1.5 miles past the North Channel Bridge to the refuge entrance, on the right. The refuge is open every day (except Thanksgiving, Christmas, and New Year's Day) from 8:30 AM to 5 PM. A permit (free) can be obtained at the visitors' center desk. Restrooms and picnic tables are located at the visitors' center; there is also a small bookshop.

The trail around the West Pond is hard-packed gravel, and suitable for wheelchairs.

Trail

The main trail circles the West Pond. Most people check the visitors' book just outside the visitors' center to see what "hot" birds have been recently seen. The first stop along the trail is an overlook onto South Marsh. This is usually a good place to find clapper rail—once we saw four of them here at once! Snowy and great egrets are here as well, and yellow-crowned night heron may also be seen. Look, too, for tricolored (Louisiana) and little blue herons. In fact, eleven species of heron, egret, and bittern are found at Jamaica Bay. This marshy area and the phragmites at station #2 are the best places to find them.

The willows along the trail provide perches for songbirds: northern mockingbird, brown thrasher, rufous-sided towhee, and house finch. On the other side of the path, the tall pines are favorite roosts for owls.

Much of the pathway here, and farther ahead, is lined with pink and white rugosa roses. Their delightful scent perfumes the air all summer. Songbirds love to build their nests in among the brambles, and the rose hips, produced in fall, are a favorite food of mockingbirds. Brown thrashers also eat these fruits. Although mockingbirds are known to be great songsters and mimics, the brown thrasher has more songs than any other U.S. bird—over 1,000!

Stops at benches #2, 3, 4, and 5 overlook part of the West Pond and the phragmites. This 45-acre freshwater pond (along with the 100-acre East Pond) was constructed in 1951. Robert Moses, then New York City Parks Commissioner, had the idea to create this refuge. In 1953, Herbert Johnson, a Parks Department employee, was transferred to Jamaica Bay and became the first refuge manager. Johnson transformed the barren landscape of Ruler's Bar Hassock— the main island—into the haven for birds and other wildlife that it is today.

In winter, the West Pond is a mecca for ducks, and one can easily see hundreds of bay ducks: canvasback, ruddy, lesser scaup, and American wigeon. The unusual Eurasian wigeon often makes an appearance, once a season. On the other side, in Black Wall Channel, you can see sea ducks: bufflehead, red-breasted merganser, and greater scaup.

The West Pond in summer

From station #8 a dirt path makes a small loop west to what is known as the tern nesting area, even though terns haven't nested there for over twenty years. In fall this is an excellent place for shorebirds: Hudsonian and marbled godwits can be seen here—statuesque cinnamon-colored birds, with long, upturned bills. The best way to tell them apart is that the Hudsonian shows a white rump patch in flight, while the marbled does not. In spring, the tern nesting area is a reliable spot to find the American oystercatcher. You can usually hear its whistle from a long way off. These large brown, black, and white birds have huge orange bills that match their orange eye rings. In the winter, a snowy owl—that denizen of the Arctic—sometimes is found in this area. Must be good hunting for voles and mice in the beach grass.

The "detour" rejoins the main path at the willow grove. Black-crowned night-herons frequently roost in these willows, while common moorhens—related to rails—can be seen poking around the base of the phragmites. Moorhens are dark blue with a red shield around their bills. Double-crested cormorants often hang out on a nearby dead log, drying their wings.

As you go along the West Marsh, keep your eyes out for herons and plovers. Plovers are small, chunky shorebirds. The common ones here are the gray (formerly called black-bellied) and the semipalmated. The semipalmated (named for the way its toes are formed) is a brown and white bird, about 7 inches long, with a single ring around its neck. If you see a larger (10-inch) bird, with two rings, it's a killdeer. Gray plovers are bigger yet (11½ inches) with black bellies and faces, a white ruff around the shoulders, and a black-and-white speckled back. Very fine looking birds, they are.

Station #11 is another good place for rails: clapper and Virginia. Both are famously secretive. Look for a large (14-inch) wading bird with a cocked-up tail, fairly long bill, barring on the back and flanks, and white undertail. That's the clapper. The Virginia is a smaller (9-inch) version, with somewhat darker coloring. Even more uncommon is the tiny sora (8 inches). Brownish olive with a bright yellow bill, it, too, has the characteristic cocked-up tail.

After leaving the pond area, you come to a T-intersection. To the right are the gardens and the visitors' center. For several years, a northern saw-whet owl wintered in a dense conifer here. A good way to find roosting owls is to look for a white wash on the tree trunks. Or look for pellets on the ground. The pellets—an inch or so long—are the undigested remains of an owl's meal. They usually contain the bones and hair of its prey, a shrew, mouse, or vole. The only owl known to nest at the refuge is the barn owl, and the nest-box program has been quite productive. Over fifty young barn owls were banded in the mid-1980s. Although owls are more easily seen in winter, any and all sightings are rare.

The North and South Gardens have an informal network of paths through them. Butterfly boxes have been erected in the gardens, and plantings were established to attract butterflies. Some of these plants include buddleia, butterflyweed, and milkweed—the preferred food of monarch butterflies. About fifty species of butterflies have now been recorded at Jamaica Bay. Among them are black and tiger swallowtails, checkered white, American copper, spring azure, mourning cloak, American painted lady, buckeye, red admiral, red-spotted purple, and least skipper.

You may prefer to stay on the gravel trail that parallels the gardens and leads through a piney area, good for palm warblers. This songbird has a red cap and is yellow below; it's often found on the ground, bobbing its tail. Then continue past a bird blind back to the visitors' center.

In springtime, it's usually best to bird the gardens early and then go around the pond. Warblers are more active early in the morning, so you have a better chance of spotting them.

For the hardy, there is access to the East Pond, which is on the other side of Cross Bay Boulevard. As you leave the refuge, turn left (north) and walk about ½ mile to a path on the right. This will take you to Big John's Pond and into the East Garden, which overlooks the East Pond. Additionally, a small, poorly defined trail goes from Cross Bay Boulevard to the south end of the pond. Be sure to wear waterproof boots since a good portion of the trail is along the edge of the water. It is possible to take the trail nearly all the way around the East Pond—from the East Garden toward the north, and come out off the South Flats (or vice versa). Most good shorebirding can be done, however, by simply visiting the South Flats and walking around to The Raunt, an area of pilings near the eastern side of the pond. Be sure to bring insect repellent.

Though natural in appearance, the water level in the East Pond is controlled, and is lowered from June to September to provide mudflats for migrating shorebirds. Many thousands of birds stop here to feed and rest while migrating southward along the Atlantic Flyway. Lowering the water level also permits visitor access to the pond. During high water, you can visit only the trailhead in the East Garden.

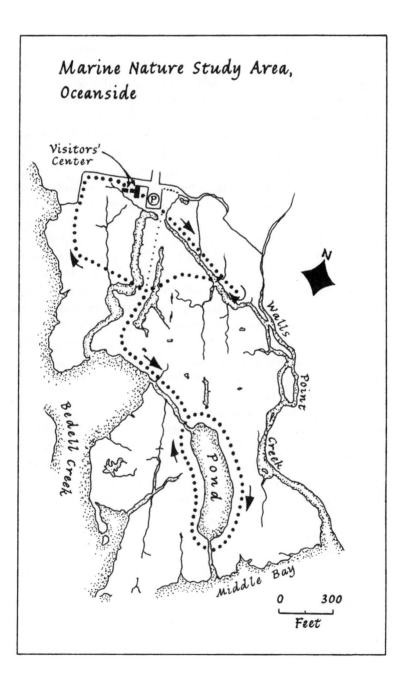

Marine Nature Study Area,
Oceanside

Visitors'
Center

P

N

Walls Point Creek

Bedell Creek

Pond

Middle Bay

0   300
Feet

Marine Nature
Study Area

Location: Oceanside
Owner: Town of Hempstead,
Department of Conservation and Waterways
Distance: 1 mile

The Marine Nature Study Area is a fifty-two-acre marshland. Part of the outwash plain, this area is characterized by salt marsh, tidal creeks, and a small upland area. The study area is truly a remnant of what once existed all over Long Island's south shore. It's wedged between a golf course, a housing development, and a solid waste center. But even though people are all around, nature prevails here. This is a small window on a world that isn't usually accessible.

Staff biologists monitor the waterways and the ecology of the salt marsh. Plant and animal life thrive in this corner of calm. Salt meadow grass, salt marsh cordgrass, greenbrier, rugosa rose, sassafras, sea rocket, bayberry, and beach plum provide habitat for diamondback terrapin, sharp-tailed sparrow, clapper rail, osprey, and a variety of fish and marine invertebrates.

Access

From Meadowbrook Parkway take the Sunrise Highway exit west. Go 1.9 miles to Milburn Avenue, turn left (south) and go 1.1 miles to Atlantic Avenue. Turn right (west) and continue 0.9 mile to Waukena Avenue, turn left on Waukena and go 0.7 mile to Park Drive. Turn left on Park Drive, go 0.3 mile to Golf Drive, turn left again, and follow the signs through the development to the sanctuary. The study area is open Monday through Friday year-round, on Saturdays from April through October, on Sundays from February through November. There is no admission charge. A visitors' center

The salt marsh

houses restrooms and exhibits about the study area. Picnic tables are located by the parking lot, under a stand of trees.

The boardwalks and trails are wheelchair accessible. For information, call 516-766-1580.

Trail

The mile-long, self-guiding trail (booklet available in the visitors' center) begins at the parking lot, and at first you'll come to a boardwalk over the salt marsh. This area is characterized by salt marsh cordgrass and salt meadow grass. In the nearby housing developments the native vegetation has all been cut away, but here nature can take its course. Clapper rails are denizens of the salt marsh. They build their nests in a firm bank, occasionally under a small bush. Lucky observers can see this secretive wading bird as it moves deliberately through the narrow channels, pecking at the mud in search of crustaceans, worms, snails, even small frogs, to eat.

Some of these channels are natural (the ones that meander). The straight ones are drainage ditches, cut to help control the mosquito population. Other birds that find food in these channels include great and snowy egrets, little blue heron, spotted sandpiper, willet, and greater and lesser yellowlegs. Since both yellowlegs species sport the yellow legs for which they are named, the best way to tell them apart is to examine their bills; the greater yellowlegs' bill is much larger in relation to its head than the bill of the lesser yellowlegs. Snowy and great egrets, too, have many similarities, and although the snowy is smaller than the great, the size difference isn't always apparent. The great egret has a yellow-orange bill, whereas the snowy's bill is black. Their feet are different, too (the great has black feet while the snowy shows its "golden slippers" when it flies), but this can be difficult to see when the bird is standing in water. The willet is easy to identify, especially when you hear it call its "pee-wee-willet" whistle. In flight, its white wing flashes are also diagnostic.

The small bird flying about the marsh in great numbers is the lovely tree swallow. These birds nest in the boxes placed in the salt marsh, and are frequently seen just sitting atop their homes or on the boardwalk rail. Often they allow you to get quite close. Their plumage is dazzling: pure white beneath, iridescent blue above.

Farther along on the boardwalk is an elevated platform. This will give you a good overview of the marsh, as you're able to look directly down into the dense cordgrass. Dragonflies—those "living flashes of light," according to Tennyson—sail low over the marsh.

The boardwalk loop then joins the path and you continue to the pond. In the phragmites here, Canada geese make their nests, often quite close to the path. They can be belligerent at times, defending their nests, eggs, and chicks. This is also a good place to find sharp-tailed sparrows—small birds with short, pointed tails and boldly patterned heads. Look for a bright orange triangle around a dark ear patch. The more common song sparrow has a central breast spot and a long, rounded tail.

Once you get to the end of the pond, you're overlooking Middle Bay, near the outflow of Bedell Creek. Just across the bay you can see osprey nesting platforms. These platforms, atop tall poles, have been instrumental in returning nesting osprey to Long Island. The platforms, and now breeding osprey as well, can be seen all over Long Island's coastal areas. Osprey dive feet first into the water, often coming up with a fish in their talons. They carry their prey—like a torpedo—calling "kip, kip, kip" all the way to the nest. While incubating their clutch, usually of two or three eggs, the female is fed entirely by her mate. The eggs take five to six weeks to hatch, and then the chicks need to be fed, too. Both parents take part in feeding their young, each one of which needs about two pounds of fish daily. Osprey mate for life, and return each year to refurbish their nest of the previous year, so the nests sometimes become quite large and ungainly.

Back along the other side of the pond you overlook Bedell Creek. In winter and early spring this is a good place to find brant, the smaller, darker cousin of the Canada goose. Wintering ducks here include red-breasted merganser, gadwall, northern pintail, greater scaup, and bufflehead.

A left turn at the intersection takes you over a small bridge and into the upland area of the preserve. Here the sweet perfumes of wild and rugosa roses vie with each other. Yellow warblers hang out in the eastern redcedars, as do house finches and northern flickers. Many warblers pass through on spring and fall migration, but the yellow nests here. On the way back to the visitors' center, look for mockingbirds on the lawn.

Sands Point
Preserve

Location: Port Washington
Owner: Nassau County
Distance: about 1 mile

O nce upon a time, before there were taxes, the wheelers and dealers of this country put their newly acquired millions into building castles, villas, and châteaux along the North Shore of Long Island. It was a world of magnificence and indulgence, of the tasteful and the tawdry—and it was the inspiration for that classic novel of the Jazz Age, *The Great Gatsby.*

One of the highlights of this Gold Coast era was the Howard Gould estate. The son of notorious railroad tycoon Jay Gould, Howard Gould built a gothic home, fashioned after Ireland's Kilkenny Castle, and constructed both a massive stable and a carriage house. In 1917, the property was bought by Daniel Guggenheim, a copper magnate, who named the residence Hempstead House. His son, Harry, used ninety acres of the property to create the Falaise estate in 1923. It is believed that *Gatsby*'s West Egg is, in fact, Sands Point. To add to the fame, Charles Lindbergh, who was a good friend of Harry Guggenheim, stayed at Falaise after his celebrated flight across the Atlantic. Meanwhile, Guggenheim and his wife, Alicia Patterson, founded the Long Island paper *Newsday.* And, last but not least, part of *The Godfather* was filmed at Falaise.

So it's pretty hard to grasp that, with all these historical connections, there's also a lovely nature preserve here with six trails, a freshwater pond, and even a small nature center. Lying along the Harbor Hill glacial moraine that extends out along the North Shore, Sands Point Preserve is a blend of mature mixed forest, lawns reverting to wildflower-filled meadows, and rocky coastal shoreline with nesting bank swallows.

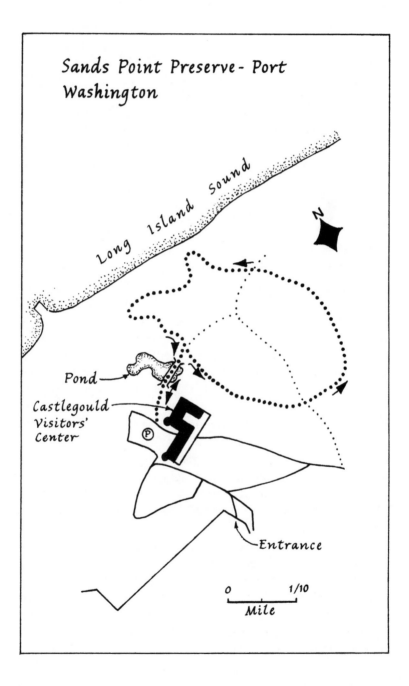

Sands Point Preserve - Port Washington

Long Island Sound

N

Pond

Castlegould
Visitors'
Center

Entrance

0   1/10
Mile

Access

From the intersection of NY 25A (Northern Boulevard) and NY 101, take NY 101 (Port Washington Boulevard) north 4.8 miles to Sands Point Preserve. The entrance is on the right.

The preserve is open daily 10 AM to 5 PM. Restrooms are located in the visitors' center, in Castlegould.

Tours of Falaise and Hempstead House are offered in the afternoon, Wednesday to Sunday, from the beginning of May to the end of October. For information, call 516-571-7900.

Trail

There's probably no other preserve with such an elegant entryway as Sands Point. You begin at Castlegould, the former stables, and follow the markers to trail #4, down a slight incline. You pass wisteria and walk along the road as it crosses over the southern end of the pond. This 1½-acre pond is so choked with duckweed that there's little water visible. A tiny plant that grows on the surface of slow-moving water, duckweed is indeed relished by ducks. In fact, if you are lucky, you may catch a glimpse of what has to be North America's most beautiful waterbird—the wood duck.

The male wood duck sports a green head patterned with white stripes and a slicked-back crest. Its green-and-white head, white throat, cinnamon chest speckled with white, and long square tail make it easily recognizable. Its female companion may be duller in color but has a prominent white eye ring that extends back in a teardrop shape. The pair nest in tree cavities or in the nesting boxes that you often see standing on a pole at the edge of a pond. Wood ducks are shy, and tend to keep to the edges of a pond. They'll quickly swim out of view if disturbed, so you need to be very quiet to observe them.

Look here also for the more familiar mallards and perhaps some turtles sunning themselves on floating logs. In the thickets surrounding the pond, listen for catbirds and robins. Cedar waxwings and scarlet tanagers are here in fall; in spring the area is a favorite stop for migrating warblers. And in summer, you may see a belted kingfisher or an eastern phoebe, the latter a flycatcher with a gray back, white underparts, and dark head. Its habit of wagging its tail when it lands on a perch is a clue to its identity. Phoebes are fairly common birds in a woodland, though their plain appearance means they usually don't catch the casual walker's eye. Be thankful, however, that the bird spends most of its day catching mosquitoes.

Trail #4 begins at the path to the right, after the bridge. Follow the trail past an area with a ground cover of myrtle, or periwinkle. Myrtle, a member of the dogbane family, is a low, trailing evergreen plant with purplish blue flowers. An introduced plant, it is here as an escape from cultivated areas of the estate. The trees in this woodland are largely black and white oaks, birch, red maple, flowering dogwood, and sassafras. There's also lots of honeysuckle, spicebush, and mapleleaf viburnum. Spicebush is easiest to identify in very early spring, when its mustard yellow flowers bloom in tight clusters against the bare branches. Later in the season, the long, dark green leaves of the spicebush have a spicy fragrance when crushed. The twigs and leaves of this lovely native shrub are used to make a tea.

The wildflowers of Sands Point are best seen in spring and early summer and include Canada mayflower, mayapple, jack-in-the-pulpit, Solomon's seal and false Solomon's seal, and wild geranium. New York, lady, and Christmas ferns grow in the understory and along the path. One day on this trail we came across a stand of Indian pipe.

Lacking chlorophyll, the saprophytic Indian pipe arises unexpectedly from decaying material in the soil. The scaled stems—the scales are actually its leaves—are erect, each supporting a single flower that bends downward, giving the appearance of a churchwarden pipe stuck in the ground. John Turner, in his book *Exploring the Other Island,* says that this plant has also been called dead man's fingers, because the bunch of stalks can resemble the upright hand of a buried person clawing his way to the surface. He adds that Indian pipe is also called convulsion weed because of its emetic properties. Quite a versatile plant, since it was once prescribed as a remedy for eye irritations. Indian pipe doesn't last long; it's gone almost as soon as it appears.

Also along this trail—and certainly of a more permanent nature—are several glacial erratics. These large, rounded boulders have

Castlegould—the visitors' center

traveled far; most likely they were brought here from Canada by the last glacier and dropped when the glacier was retreating and lightening its load, so to speak. The North Shore of Long Island has lots of erratics—Shelter Rock, just south of Northern Boulevard in Manhasset, is one of the largest.

The trail soon turns to the left and follows a steep-sided valley, with a preserve road passing overhead. This valley was carved by a stream of glacial meltwater. The hillsides are lush with holly and rhododendrons. American holly grows sparingly in New England and New York, where it is always small. Its pretty white flowers appear in clusters along the stems, while the berries are the familiar scarlet. The rhodies are rosebay rhododendron, a native species that once grew in woods throughout Long Island but has for the most part now disappeared.

As the trail curves left, you will rise up out of the valley. The woods here are generously sprinkled with the lacy mapleleaf viburnum, one of our most attractive native shrubs. Note the maple leaf–shaped leaves, a dead giveaway for identification, but also recognize the plant by its flat layers of white, clustered flowers. In fall, the leaves turn a lovely purple-pink and the purple-black berries are a favorite food of mockingbirds and catbirds.

Follow along through the open woodland until you leave the tall trees and enter an area largely of sumacs. Sumacs belong to the cashew family, a group of mostly tropical plants. Several members of this family are known irritants; poison ivy is one, poison sumac another. These sumacs, however, are winged and smooth sumacs, two sun-loving species that colonize an area that has been disturbed. When the surrounding trees shade the area, the sumacs will die. Spindly, awkward trees, the sumacs are really only attractive when leafed out, and especially in fall, when the leaves turn scarlet. The leaves of the winged sumac are hairy, with a winged midrib between the leaflets. The smooth sumac's twigs have a whitish bloom, which distinguishes it from its cousins. (Poison sumac looks entirely different—rather like a dogwood with hanging clusters of white berries.) Sumac fruits are supposedly rich in vitamin A.

The trail continues to an overlook, where you will have brilliant views of Long Island Sound and Hempstead Harbor. On a clear day you can see Westchester and Connecticut. It's easy to see how this beach of boulders has been eroded by wave action. Though the sound isn't as powerful as the ocean, it slowly cuts away at the shore, piling debris from the cliff at the shoreline and drawing sand out to sea. In addition to the bank swallows flying in and out of their burrows in the cliff, you will likely see cormorants swimming near shore, while gulls and terns fish from the air.

Return from the overlook and thread your way back to the woodland through a child's play world of arches and tangles. Many of the trees here are ailanthus—the tree that grows in Brooklyn also grows on Long Island. Also called the tree-of-heaven, ailanthus is a rugged colonizer of waste areas and disturbed woodlands. A native of China, its seeds were sent to England in 1751 by Jesuit missionaries, who believed that it could be used to grow silkworms there. The tree soon made its way to North America, where it lost favor because of its smelly blossoms. Nevertheless, it has virtues: ailanthus is highly tolerant of air pollution, its foliage is bright green and lush through the summer, and in fall the leaves turn lemon yellow. Because it's not fussy, it will grow almost anywhere, in the poorest of soil.

Shortly, the trail comes out onto the road, just beyond the bridge and pond where you began. Return to the stables and, if you have time, take a tour of Hempstead House or Falaise for contrast.

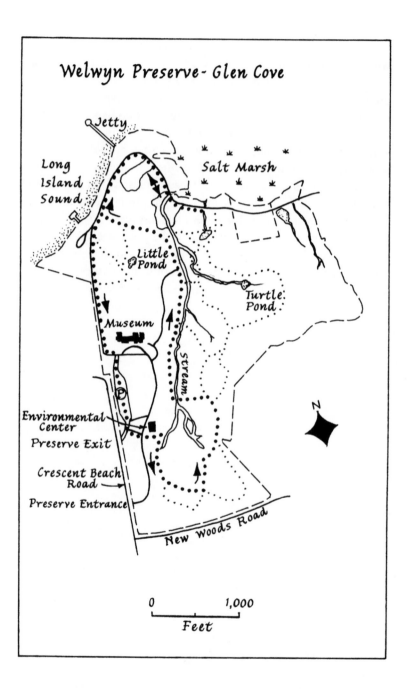

Welwyn Preserve - Glen Cove

Jetty

Long Island Sound

Salt Marsh

Little Pond

Turtle Pond

Museum

Stream

Environmental Center

Preserve Exit

Crescent Beach Road

Preserve Entrance

New Woods Road

N

0   1,000

Feet

Welwyn Preserve

Location: Glen Cove
Owner: Nassau County
Distance: 1–1½ miles

When you walk into Welwyn Preserve you walk into the past. Welwyn is the 200-acre former estate of Harold Irving Pratt, son of Charles Pratt, an oil magnate and philanthropist of the late 1800s. It's one of six Pratt family estates that occupied an 800-acre stretch of Long Island's Gold Coast, a region once famous for its lavish homes and glamorous 1920s society. The 1912 Georgian-style mansion is now Nassau County's Holocaust Museum; the grounds have been a nature sanctuary since 1980 and will continue as such.

The natural splendor of this property will be immediately evident as you pass through a gracious stone gateway and into a grove of sky-high tulip trees and spreading rhododendrons. One of the county's lesser-known wild spots, Welwyn is usually quiet, save for the rustle of squirrels or the call of chickadees. The extensive trails pass through an unusually rich and diverse habitat for this region, from woodlands, streams, and a freshwater pond, to saltwater marsh and coastal beach. Visit it in all seasons, although spring is an especially good time to see migrating warblers and early streamside wildflowers.

Access

From the Long Island Expressway (I-495), take exit 39, Glen Cove Road North. Go north on Glen Cove Road 6.2 miles (bearing left at a major fork) to the end of the road. Turn right onto Brewster Street; go 0.5 mile. Then turn left onto Dosoris Lane; go 0.7 mile to New Woods Road. Turn left and go 0.4 mile to a T-intersection with Crescent Beach Road. Turn right on Crescent Beach. The entrance gate is the first driveway on the right. The preserve is open Wednesday through Sunday, 9:30 AM to 4:30 PM.

Trail

Walk back from the parking lot toward the entrance, passing a small office building on the left. Black-capped chickadee, white-breasted nuthatch, and house finch are common visitors to the birdfeeders here, but it is always worth checking for something more unusual. The trail begins on the far side of the building, and maps are available in a small box at the trailhead.

The first thing you'll notice is the detour. A fire some years ago burned most of the building in back, so the trail now goes south for a while, beside the stream, then crosses over and parallels the stream in reverse direction, before returning to the original trail #1.

As you pass beneath these towering tulip trees, consider that Welwyn is far more than the remnant of an extinct lifestyle. Here also is a fragment of Long Island's mostly vanished natural history—a stand of trees that have never been cut; ponds that formed naturally, when the last glacier retreated; wildflowers that have grown here since people first walked these lands. The tulip tree was once common on Long Island, from Brooklyn to Stony Brook, but many of them, particularly those on the North Shore, were cut in the 1800s to furnish New York City with high-grade lumber. Here at Welwyn is one of the last remaining stands of old-growth tulip trees on Long Island. And these tulip trees are truly magnificent, some exceeding 14 feet in diameter and standing 100 feet tall. In late spring you'll notice the trail littered with spent tulip tree flowers—about 1½ inches long, with six light yellow-green petals, tinged with orange at the base. Glance up at the treetops in fall after the leaves have fallen, and you'll see the skeletons of flowers that didn't drop in spring.

This beginning section of trail gives you the best overview of a mixed mesophytic forest, comprising not only tulip tree but also American beech, mockernut hickory, and hemlock. Because Long Island is a meeting ground of two biological life zones (Carolinian and Canadian), there exists here a rich diversity of plant species, despite the fact that there are no major geologic features. When the glacier retreated, the first species to grow on Long Island were the colder-climate trees and shrubs. As the climate became milder, species likely to be found farther south migrated north. Thus, the "northern" hemlock and the "southern" tulip tree grow side by side.

The trail follows a trickle of a stream. You may well spot a black-throated blue warbler in the lower branches of a yellow birch or hear the drum of a hairy woodpecker. In early spring the west-facing slope is covered with the young yellow-green leaves of emerging skunk cabbage. Though you would find its odor off-putting should you crush a leaf, the plant uses that scent to lure insects to its flower, thus helping ensure pollination. A more pleasant prospect is the mass of blooming trout lilies. Also called dogtooth violet, this delicate spring wildflower arises pertly from a pair of brownish mottled basal leaves.

As you leave the high woods, and the stream grows wider and begins to meander, you'll come to an intersection. Trail #1 turns right and goes across the stream. At this point, continue straight ahead, now following trail #2. To the left is a stand of Japanese knotweed, an alien species and not an attractive one, either. Also intruding here are a few cultivated species such as myrtle, or periwinkle. This low evergreen trailing vine with a lovely star-shaped blue flower is a common ground cover in gardens, and it has grown into the preserve from the nearby carriage house. In other parts of the preserve you'll see occasional daffodils, azaleas, tea roses, and the like. In their days, the Pratts had a well-tended garden. It's ironic that in a garden we pluck out as weeds our native plants, while cultivated ones escape our gardens to settle in wild areas.

Look up to the left as you pass the knotweed, or climb the ridge along the side path to view the meadow above. This area, once lawn and orchard, is now heavily draped in vines—ivy, euonymous, wild grape, Virginia creeper, bittersweet, honeysuckle, and poison ivy. The Virginia creeper has small suction cups at the end of its wiry tendrils; the bittersweet and honeysuckle entwine themselves around trees; and the others grasp onto vegetation with their hairlike aerial roots. Be especially quiet and you might see a gray catbird or Carolina wren pop up and sing, or spy a white-throated sparrow or rufous-sided towhee scratching the ground for seeds.

Return to the trail and continue along the stream. This stream, which runs north toward Long Island Sound, is fed by underground

Freshwater stream

springs in the area. Unlike many other streams on Long Island, this one runs throughout the year. Nearby you'll see moisture-loving striped maple and sassafras, as well as Canada mayflower, starflower, and Solomon's seal. There are more yellow birch here, too, because that tree prefers the moist soil of a mature upland forest. Since its seeds germinate easily in the soft soil around a decaying stump, the saplings often wrap their roots around these stumps, giving the appearance of being perched.

In the shallow pools of the stream are water striders—insects about an inch long that skim the surface for smaller insects to eat. Water striders hibernate near shore and return to the water on the first warm day of spring. Pickerel frogs can sometimes be seen here, too.

At this point, trail #2 turns right and crosses the stream. If you have time, take #2 a short way to get a view of freshwater Turtle Pond. There's a river birch tree here, extremely rare for Long Island, and always the chance to see the resident belted kingfisher. Then return to the trail intersection.

If you keep on straight, following trail #3, shortly it will skirt a grove of tall hemlocks and white pines. During a recent winter storm, many of the trees were knocked down, so the center of the grove is inaccessible. But as you pass the pines, check the treetops for great horned owls. They regularly nest here and can be seen by the sharp-eyed. Look high up for white wash on a tree trunk, a good sign that a roosting owl may be nearby. With eyes over thirty-five times more sensitive than a human's, and the most acute hearing of any animal, the great horned owl will most certainly be watching you.

The path continues to the water, with a sweeping view of Long Island Sound and the remnants of the Pratts', once-gracious cast-iron pier. If you turn right and follow the path around the piles of cement, you'll come to the salt marsh, where, in summer, there are likely to be snowy egrets and great blue herons. The osprey nesting platform generally hosts a pair, as Long Island populations gradually recover from near extinction (which was due to DDT spraying and habitat loss).

Returning to the shore and continuing alongside a small stand of Austrian black pines, you'll notice the wild beach plum, rosa rugosa, and prickly pear (a native cactus). The path is then joined by a road that will return you to the parking lot. On your way back, try a few of the paths that branch off to the left. Some will take you back into the pine grove and to Little Pond, where the wood thrush's fluty song echoes all spring.

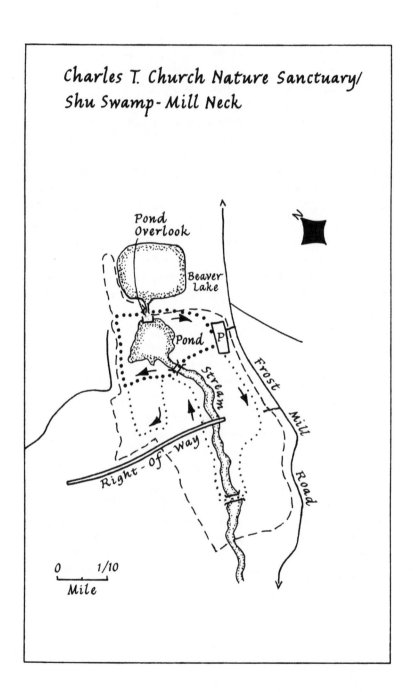

Charles T. Church Nature Sanctuary/ Shu Swamp- Mill Neck

Pond Overlook

Beaver Lake

Pond

P

Stream

Frost Mill Road

Right-of-Way

0   1/10
Mile

Charles T. Church Nature Sanctuary/ Shu Swamp

Location: Mill Neck
Owner: The North Shore Wildlife Sanctuary, Inc.
Distance: 1 mile

ur first nature walk on Long Island was a visit to Shu Swamp with the poet May Swenson.

Shu Swamp, Spring

Young skunk
cabbages all over
the swamp.

Brownish purple,
yellow-speckled
short tusks,

they thicken,
twirl and point
like thumbs.

Thumbs of old
gloves, the nails
poked through

and curled.
By Easter, fingers
will have flipped out

fat and green.
Old gloves, brown
underground,

the seams split.
The nails
have been growing.
                    —May Swenson

Access

From the intersection of Birch Hill Road and Forest Avenue, in Locust Valley, proceed east on Forest Avenue (which becomes Buckram Road, which becomes Oyster Bay Road) for 1.7 miles. Turn left (east) on Frost Mill Road, go 0.3 mile to a T-intersection, turn left again on Frost Mill Road (also known as Mill Neck Road), and continue for 0.5 mile to the sanctuary entrance, which will be on the left.

The sanctuary can also be reached by public transportation. Take the Oyster Bay line of the Long Island Railroad to the Mill Neck station. Walk down the hill and turn left; the sanctuary entrance is on the right, just after the bridge, 0.1 mile from the station.

The sanctuary is open from 7 AM to 7 PM, April through October; from 7 AM to 5 PM, November through March. It is closed Fridays. There is a parking lot, but there are no other public facilities. Please note that there is no parking on the streets of Mill Neck, nor at the railroad station, at any time.

Trail

The trail begins behind the information kiosk. As you start down the track, especially in early spring, you'll be sure to notice all the skunk cabbage. Though some people look for a robin, our first sign of spring is the skunk cabbage at Shu Swamp. Formally known as the Charles T. Church Nature Sanctuary, the swamp is our favorite annual spring pilgrimage. There, unfailingly, in early March, the hoods of the skunk cabbages can be seen poking out just about everywhere—from under last year's leaf litter, in a dark muddy patch, or right beside the trail. These primitive-looking maroon-and-green speckled spathes (as the hoods are called) protect the club-shaped spadix (or flower) hidden within. The hood helps to keep the plant warm, and it is thought that the warmth generated by the plant encourages the rapid growth of seeds. These seeds can then be dispersed early, thereby having a

Skunk cabbage emerging in spring

greater chance to germinate in a suitable spot. It must work, because vast areas of Shu Swamp are covered in skunk cabbage. As the flowers fade, huge leaves appear. When crushed or broken, both the leaves and the flowers give off a skunky smell, as reflected in the plant's Latin name—*Symplocarpus foetidus.*

Crows call and gather in the top of a tulip tree. Shu Swamp has an impressive stand of these tall trees. Highly valued for lumber—because of their straight, tall trunks—many of Long Island's tulip trees have been harvested. Luckily, this stand remains. There are two species of crow on Long Island—American and fish—really only discernible by their voices. The American crow has the common "caw, caw" call, while the smaller fish crow has a more nasal "cah" sound. This gathering is of American crows. Crows, probably the most intelligent of all our birds, have become an increasing presence on Long Island in recent years, gathering in large treetop roosts. Often crows will "mob" a hawk or owl, so when we hear them cawing, we always look up. This time they're just socializing.

Closer to us, a downy woodpecker is drumming softly on a snag, or dead tree. The tree is ringed with tiny holes, the work of the yellow-bellied sapsucker, another small woodpecker. Moss on the trailside is like velvet glistening in the sun.

The trail crosses the stream on a little wooden boardwalk. Beneath your feet you can see the tiny cress plants, their leaves rippling with the current. Off to the side, where the skunk cabbage is flourishing, it's muddy.

On the left, another trail branches off, to parallel the stream through woodlands. At the intersection, later in the spring (May or June) you can hear the "de-ar-ie come-here" song of the yellow-throated vireo. Vireos are small birds, similar to warblers, but with thicker bills. They're notoriously difficult to see, despite their piercing and repetitive calls. The yellow-throated vireo has bright yellow spectacles, throat, and breast; the belly is white, and the back olive green. It nests here high in a red maple tree.

Soon you come to an oak-beech woodland. This upland area of Shu Swamp is home to the red-bellied woodpecker, and you can often hear its raucous laugh. Other birds commonly seen here are hairy woodpecker, tufted titmouse, black-capped chickadee, hermit thrush, and veery. The hairy woodpecker looks like a downy but is a little bigger and has a larger bill; its call is also different. The hermit thrush has more breast spots than the veery, and also has a rusty tail. Their songs, too, are different. According to Richard Pough (author of *Audubon Bird Guide; Small Land Birds*): "The song [of the hermit thrush] is composed of a series of ethereal bell-like cadences of great beauty. The long, low, flutelike opening note is followed by up to a dozen shorter, thinner notes varying slightly in pitch, and run together in groups to give a tremolo effect." The veery's call note resembles its name, while its song "is a rolling series of half a dozen falling or downward-slurred muffled notes."

The trail turns to the right and follows along an old chain-link fence. The dead and down trees here are in the process of decomposition—bugs, worms, and other animals all playing their part.

As you leave the upland area, you pass through another hotbed of skunk cabbage and go on to the pond overlook. To the left (on the other side of the tracks) is Beaver Dam. An osprey has nested here in years past. The pond—although not very deep—is home to ducks and swans. Canada geese honk noisily overhead. The nesting boxes at the far end of the pond are for wood ducks, often seen here. In fall, solitary sandpipers stop off for a rest. In late spring and summer, the culvert below the bridge is a nesting area for barn swallows. These graceful, long-tailed birds zoom over the top of the pond, catching insects on the wing.

Now, in March, catkins are loaded with yellow pollen and the red maple buds are swollen. Red-winged blackbirds are busy staking out territories: "Koo-churr-ee!" they call as they flash their brilliant epaulets. Cattails are fuzzy with last year's seeds.

The trail leaves the pond and goes back through a little wooded area before returning to the parking lot.

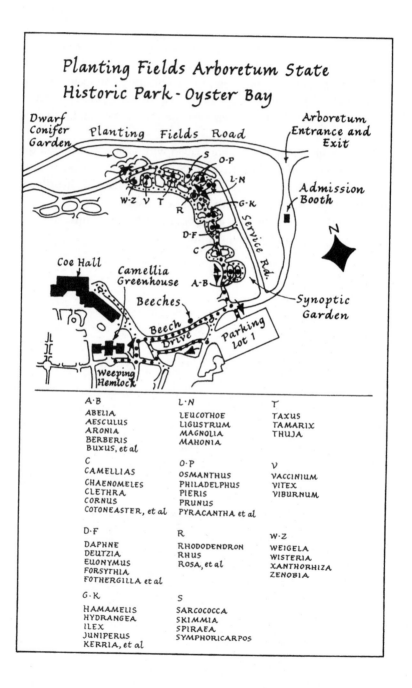

Planting Fields Arboretum State Historic Park - Oyster Bay

Dwarf Conifer Garden

Planting Fields Road

Arboretum Entrance and Exit

Admission Booth

S O·P
L·N
G·K
W·Z V T R
Service Rd.
D·F
C
A·B

N

Coe Hall

Camellia Greenhouse

Beeches

A·B

Synoptic Garden

Beech Drive

Parking Lot 1

Weeping Hemlock

A·B	L·N	T
ABELIA	LEUCOTHOE	TAXUS
AESCULUS	LIGUSTRUM	TAMARIX
ARONIA	MAGNOLIA	THUJA
BERBERIS	MAHONIA	
BUXUS, et al		
C	O·P	V
CAMELLIAS	OSMANTHUS	VACCINIUM
CHAENOMELES	PHILADELPHUS	VITEX
CLETHRA	PIERIS	VIBURNUM
CORNUS	PRUNUS	
COTONEASTER, et al	PYRACANTHA et al	
D·F	R	W·Z
DAPHNE	RHODODENDRON	WEIGELA
DEUTZIA	RHUS	WISTERIA
EUONYMUS	ROSA, et al	XANTHORHIZA
FORSYTHIA		ZENOBIA
FOTHERGILLA et al		
G·K	S	
HAMAMELIS	SARCOCOCCA	
HYDRANGEA	SKIMMIA	
ILEX	SPIRAEA	
JUNIPERUS	SYMPHORICARPOS	
KERRIA, et al		

Planting Fields
Arboretum
State Historic Park

Location: Oyster Bay
Owner: New York State
Distance: less than 1 mile

February on Long Island can be bleak—gray days, snowy trails, and bitter cold. But it's on just these days that we go walking among the camellias. In fact, the icier the better. That way, when we step into the Camellia Greenhouse at Planting Fields, the warm, humid air kisses our cheeks with the feel of summer.

Ah, the luxury of such an experience in the midst of winter. It's the bequest of William Robertson Coe, an insurance executive. Coe's 409-acre estate, including his sixty-five-room Tudor Revival mansion and his magnificent greenhouses, constitutes Planting Fields Arboretum State Historic Park. The 160 acres of Olmsted-designed gardens boast majestic beech and linden trees set against an expanse of lawn. Additionally, cedars, firs, elms, tulip trees, oaks, and magnolias grow alongside plantings of over 600 different varieties of rhododendron and azaleas.

Planting Fields has several short trails, such as the one that skirts an area of native trees and shrubs, or the woodland walk through a bird sanctuary (complete with a covered bridge, a pool, and a bird blind), or a wildflower path. In warmer seasons, all of these make fine outings, but in winter, a visit to the Camellia Greenhouse and a stroll through the Synoptic Garden are a fine way to spend an afternoon. The camellias are in bloom from mid-January through March, but the height of bloom is from mid-February through the first week of March.

Access

From the intersection of Mill River Road and NY 25A (Northern Boulevard), take Mill River Road north for 2 miles, to a sign for Planting Fields, turn left (west) onto Glen Cove Road, and go 0.4 mile to Planting Fields Road. Turn left again and proceed 0.2 mile to the entrance. Planting Fields is open daily 9 AM to 5 PM. From May 1 to Labor Day (and on Saturdays, Sundays, and holidays the rest of the year) a fee of $3 per car is charged.

The greenhouses are open from 10 AM to 4 PM. Coe Hall is open for guided tours from April through September; for information, call 516-922-0479. The visitors' center, adjacent to the main greenhouses, houses classrooms, an educational exhibit, and a gift shop; restrooms are nearby. For information about other activities—including classes (in botany, horticulture, and art), horticultural societies, and concerts—call 516-922-9200.

Trail

The Camellia Greenhouse

Enter the Camellia Greenhouse through the center door, opposite the weeping hemlock (the largest tree of its kind on Long Island). You'll immediately be overcome by the luxuriant beauty of these unfolding flowers. The double blossoms are full—a bounty of glistening petals, one upon the other, circling the center stamens. Their curls and ruffles are set upon shrubs of shiny, evergreen leaves. Walk to the left or the right of the center display area—you can't go wrong—and notice how full the bushes are with flowers and buds. Camellias go all out, setting far more flower buds than they ought to. This excess is usually trimmed by nature, as some buds drop off so the plant can put its energies into the remaining flowers-to-be.

Walk down the aisle and around the sides, and note the different shades of pink and red and white—as well as white with pink and pink or red with white—even candy stripes and polka dots. These shrubs are all of only three species, but the flowers you see are testimony to the energies of cultivators, who develop new varieties to tempt the gardener. They give them classy names, like 'Lady Clare Kelvinton', 'Prince Albert', 'Lady Marion', 'Madame Cachet', 'Lady

Vansittart', 'Duke of Devonshire', and 'Duchess of Sutherland'. Then there are the mysterious names, like 'Sawada's Dream', and the dramatic names, like 'Blood of China.'

Camellias are members of the tea family (Theaceae) and native to China and Japan. They were a favorite flower of the Orient and then of Europe, from where they were brought to the New World in the 1700s. In short order, they became a popular plant in southern U.S. gardens, where the climate suited their growing needs.

Many of the camellias in this greenhouse are *Camellia japonica,* generally termed the common camellia (although its flowers are far from common!). Also here is the *Camellia reticulata,* or Chinese camellia. The cultivar 'Captain Rawes' was for many years quite rare, with six of the nine mature plants in the country located here at the Coe estate. (Mr. Coe ran a small business selling cuttings of these plants.) The third species, *Camellia sasanqua,* has a leggier appearance; the only variety here of this species is 'Cleopatra.'

Is there something missing from this flower show? Yes. Sniff a camellia blossom and you'll detect little or no scent. The sweet fragrance you catch in the air may well be coming from *Daphne odora,* a more modest evergreen shrub that is grown in parts of the greenhouse. When the lavish beauty of a camellia is nearby, other plants just have to try a little harder.

The Synoptic Garden

From the Camellia Greenhouse, walk along Beech Drive back toward the entrance to Planting Fields. As you pass the stand of tall beech trees underplanted with rhododendrons, you'll reach a path on the left with a small building to its right. This is the entrance to the Synoptic Garden. The name comes from *synopsis,* in that the garden is a synopsis of desirable ornamental plants. The path winds round in an arc, with loops off to the left and right that you can choose to follow as the mood suits you.

Plants in the Synoptic Garden are arranged alphabetically by genus, so the beginning of the trail features those whose genus, or scientific surname, is *Abelia* or *Aronia* or *Bergeris,* and so on. Although this might at first seem a strange arrangement for a garden, it is

Entrance to the Synoptic Garden

exceptionally helpful for gardeners. One of Mr. Coe's requirements when he deeded the land to the state was that the property be used for educational purposes. The Synoptic Garden is a pleasant way to get to know the scientific names for some common plants.

In February, much of the garden is dormant, but the bare branches reveal some otherwise hidden beauties of nature. Note the shredding cinnamon brown bark of the cutleaf maple *(Acer griseum)* and the

Japanese clethra *(Clethra barbinervis)*. In the "C" section, look also for the different types of decorative dogwoods (*Cornus* genus)—some have bright yellow branches, others bright red. Winter is also a good time to appreciate the twists and turns of the Harry Lauder Walking Stick (*Corylus avellana* 'Contorta') and the corkscrew willow (*Salix matsudana* 'Tortuosa').

Snowy, cold days are the prime time to notice the evergreens, of course. The rhododendrons will likely be curling their leaves, a moisture-retaining reaction to the cold air. Some shrubs—such as the hollies, skimmia, and sweet box—are apt to still have their fruits. The berries of the viburnums and dogwoods are especially popular with mockingbirds.

The bright, wispy flowers of the witch hazel might well be blooming when you're here in February. There are several varieties of witch hazel *(Hamamelis)* at Planting Fields. Perhaps the most dramatic is 'Arnold's Promise', but note also the red witch hazels—the flowers don't stand out as much but they are equally fascinating. And give a sniff to the Chinese witch hazels—these are some of the most fragrant.

In March, you may see some early-flowering Cornelian cherries (a type of dogwood; *Cornus mas* and *Cornus officinalis*). And if there's been a warm spell, it's possible that there will be snowdrops *(Galanthus nivalis)*, winter aconites *(Eranthis hyemalis)*, and crocus *(Crocus)* blooming. The Lenten rose *(Helleborus orientalis)* might well be sporting its white or pink flowers already, too.

A walk through the Synoptic Garden will land you at a service road, across from the Dwarf Conifer Garden. Also good viewing in winter, this garden may be showing the first blue flowers of the tiny *Hyacinthus azureur*. To return to the parking lot, you'll have to retrace your steps along the main path of the Synoptic Garden. There's so much to learn along the way that a second view is always welcomed.

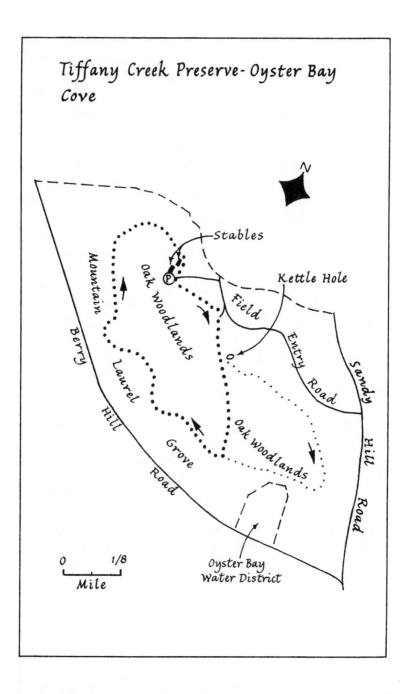

Tiffany Creek Preserve- Oyster Bay Cove

Stables

Kettle Hole

Mountain

Oak Woodlands

Field

Berry

Entry Road

Laurel

O

Hill

Sandy

Grove

Oak Woodlands

Road

Hill

Road

0   1/8
Mile

Oyster Bay
Water District

Tiffany Creek Preserve

Location: Oyster Bay Cove
Owner: Nassau County, Department of Recreation and Parks
Distance: 1 mile

T iffany Creek gives you a feeling of spaciousness, of elegance, that is otherwise hard to come by in suburban Long Island. Here, just a few miles from busy, crowded Oyster Bay, is a true retreat. It's made even lovelier by the huge stand of mountain laurel and the exquisite song of the wood thrush. As you drive into Tiffany Creek any morning in May or early June, you're likely to hear the bird's melodious song, "ee-oh-lay, ee-oh-lay," echoing throughout the woodland.

Access

From NY 25A (Northern Boulevard) in East Norwich, take NY 106 north to Oyster Bay. Turn right (east) on East Main Street, and go about 0.5 mile to Sandy Hill Road. Turn right (south) and proceed 1 mile to the preserve entrance. There are, as yet, no public facilities. For additional information, call the Muttontown Nature Center, 516-571-8500.

Trail

Tiffany Creek Preserve is made up of three former estates, now totaling nearly 200 acres of watershed lands. As of 1995, only the forty-five-acre parcel west of Sandy Hill Road has been developed for recreational use. Here, a mile-long trail traverses the oak uplands, kettle holes, and a breathtaking stand of mountain laurel *(Kalmia latifolia)*.

The parking area is next to the former stables. As you begin your walk through the woodland, you first come to an edge habitat

Pink lady's slipper

(where the forest meets a meadow), known as an ecotone. Ecotones are always areas of great diversity, and you can look here for both forest and field birds: northern mockingbird, gray catbird, brown thrasher, wood thrush, ovenbird, field sparrow, and house finch.

There are houses for eastern bluebirds in the meadow. And what could be lovelier than their special shade of blue (on the back) combined with their rusty breasts? Bluebirds are cavity nesters, and the cutting and removal of dead trees combined with stiff competition from house sparrows and European starlings have severely decimated their populations—down 90 percent from a century ago. Until a few years ago, bluebirds had been very scarce on Long Island. However, a recent interest in them (among the fashionable East End set, for instance), along with the construction of nesting boxes in suitable habitat (meadows bordered by woodlands), has caused a revival in their Long Island population. Bluebird "trails" (a succession of nesting boxes) have been set up on the East End. Nesting birds are now found at Muttontown Preserve, as well as here at Tiffany Creek. Bluebirds are also known to nest at Connetquot River State Park Preserve.

As you pass the field and reenter the oak woodlands, you'll come upon a kettle hole. In the early spring this is full of rainwater, and provides a habitat for spring peepers. By June it's pretty well dried up.

Wood warblers are calling. Ovenbirds overhead "tsk-tsk" at us: we're too near the nest. The pair try to chase us off. Ovenbirds nest on the forest floor; their nests are roofed over with leaves or branches, and open on the side, a bit like an oven, hence their name. This large (6-inch) thrushlike warbler is most often seen walking along the ground. Its breast is streaked with dark spots, its back is brownish, and it has a russet crown. The typical song of the ovenbird is a loud, rising "teacher, teacher, teacher."

A little farther along some chipmunks scamper through the crisp oak leaves. One dives into a hole at our approach. We wait patiently and he sticks his head out.

The trail now enters the mountain laurel grove. Rarely has one shrub had so many descriptive nicknames: calicotree (for the pale pink flowers, which look like the calico skirts of some eighteenth-century child), spoonwood (because the wood is good for making small tools, like spoons), and sheep-kill (because the plant's leaves are toxic to domestic animals).

In late May and early June—*the* time to be here—the grove is abloom. Mountain laurels have a distinct shape—their trunks are twisted and their branches are wavy, forming a thicket. The folk name for a dense mountain laurel thicket, like this one, is laurel hell. Laurels have an underground spreading root system that sends up new shoots; branches that touch the ground will root. The shiny, dark leaves are evergreen; the bark and heartwood are tinged with red. An umbrella-shaped mass of blooms may hold as many as a dozen individual flowers. These cuplike blossoms are white and delicately tinged with pink. (In nurseries and garden shops you can buy mountain laurel cultivars—all sorts of variations on the original theme—dark pink with red centers, red and white, and so on. But we think nothing beats the wild laurel.)

After passing through the grove, the trail once again enters a mixed oak woodland. Look here for pink lady's slipper (also known as moccasin-flower)—one of our native orchids. This lovely pink flower blooms just before the laurel, in early May. It's easy to identify: large leaves at the base of a tall (8- to 10-inch) stalk. The flower at the top of the stalk is like a large pouch, with three petals. Although sometimes found individually alongside the path, they're often in stands of up to seventy-five plants in a moist area under the tree canopy.

Many of the plants you see in this area are not native to Long Island. Norway maple, English yew, and magnolia are woody plants that have escaped from cultivated areas and have established themselves here. Even the pachysandra, a common backyard ground cover, is an escapee. But remember, this preserve was, after all, an estate. The open woodland, just behind the stables, is a favorite haunt of American robins. Listen for their "cheer-up, cheer-ee" calls as you return to the parking area.

Muttontown Preserve

Location: East Norwich
Owner: Nassau County
Distance: 2 miles

The rolling hills and fields of the 550-acre Muttontown Preserve have both a natural and a local history. As it retreated about 15,000 years ago, ice from the last continental glacier marked the area with kettle ponds, ridges, and a gravel mound. The preserve's grassy meadows and young woodlands are old farm fields that have reverted to the wild. A stand of native persimmon trees is evidence of colonization by species that usually favor a warmer climate. And a section in the southern part of the preserve has the ruins and ivy-covered walls of a former estate.

Improbable as it may seem, in 1951, the exiled King Zog of Albania decided to live in Muttontown, on the edge of Nassau County's Gold Coast. Zog had been deposed in 1939, when Mussolini took over the small, mountainous country of Albania. Zog's dream was to move in with a busload of Albanian tenant farmers, to whom he would allocate parcels of his 267-acre estate. He built a regal sixty-two-room mansion—Knollwood—but it was never occupied, and after treasure-hunters and vandals sacked it, the building was demolished.

The preserve also encompasses the pre-Revolutionary Duryea farm and the former Winthrop mansion. There is a nature center at the entrance and adjacent is the Chelsea Estate, which is used for art exhibitions. In addition to marked nature trails, there are cross-country ski trails, bridle paths, and an equestrian center.

Access

From the intersection of NY 106 and NY 25A, go west on NY 25A for 0.1 mile to Muttontown Lane. Turn left (south) and proceed 3 blocks to the preserve entrance. Muttontown Preserve is open daily

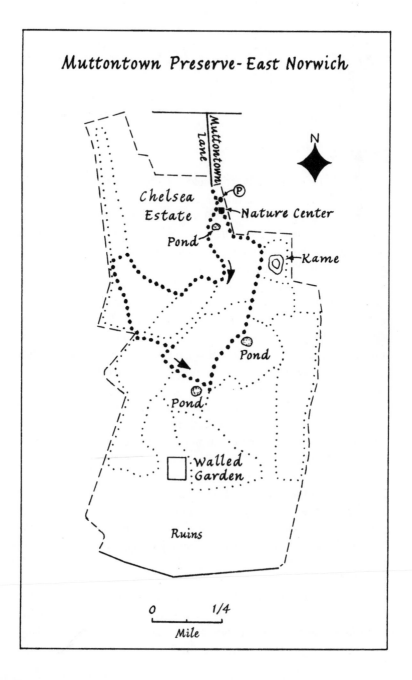

Muttontown Preserve-East Norwich

from 9:30 AM to 4:30 PM. Trail maps; checklists of birds, mammals, and plants; and restrooms are located in the Bill Paterson Nature Center.

Trail

There are many trails at Muttontown, and matching them to the map can be a challenge. But the paths have markers and, should you get lost, it isn't ever far back to the entrance. This walk goes through moist woodland and circles the central meadow, a distinguishing feature of this preserve. If you wish to visit the upland forest and ruins in the southern half of the preserve, consult the map.

Begin at the nature center, where it is likely a house wren will be declaring its territory as you approach. Walk to the right of the building and follow the signs for trail #1. You'll be passing through an open, moist woodland with tall trees—pin oak, tupelo, and red maple. Also sometimes called swamp maple, the red maple shows red on its twigs in spring, red on the leaf stems in summer, and red buds in winter. In autumn, the leaves turn brilliant crimson. The thin understory here is mostly spicebush, arrowwood, and sweet pepperbush. On the ground are wood hyacinth, Canada mayflower, and ferns. The Canada mayflower, when in bloom, extends a white-and-green carpet over the woodland.

As the trail crosses a little stream, look for catbirds and robins in the understory and the dapper towhees scratching among the leaves on the ground. When there's a heavy infestation of tent caterpillars, you might be lucky enough to see a yellow-billed cuckoo carrying a bit of lunch to its babies. Alongside the stream, in summer, are turk's-cap lilies.

The trail turns to the right and leads into an open grassy area where vines such as bittersweet and honeysuckle, as well as wild roses, have created a tangle that is appealing to yellow warblers. These "flying dandelions" often perch in the open and give their bubbling song before shooting down into a thicket.

This field to the left is reverting to the wild. Daisies, black-eyed Susans, and goldenrod grow among the bayberries and eastern red-cedar. There are also some white pine trees, crabapple, and wild cherry. As the path winds around to the left, follow trail #4 along an

Chipmunk

allée of cedars and Scotch pines that are being crowded out by red maples and white pines. This is the natural process of succession, as species compete for available light and water.

You'll soon reach a fence with an opening. Cross over and follow trail #5 to the left, reaching the other side of the meadow. Before turning right onto trail #6, search the field for eastern bluebirds and butterflies—especially swallowtails. The eastern tiger swallowtail, a 4- to almost-6-inch butterfly, has large yellow wings with black stripes and a black terminal bar; its long tails project out from its hind wings—characteristic of all swallowtails. Listen for the explosive "ko-churr-ee" of red-winged blackbirds and the cawing of American crows. Here also, sallying out from a branch and performing its aerial acrobatics, may be an eastern kingbird. This tyrant flycatcher is dark above and white below; its orange crown spot is seldom visible. And swooping overhead will be tree swallows in pursuit of the mosquitoes and other insects that flit above the grasses.

The field is cut periodically to maintain the early stages of succession. This management ensures the sparse vegetation favored by the American woodcock, a small gamebird that nests here. In early spring woodcocks perform their unusual flight display. They fly up; circle high in the night sky while giving a constant twittering call; and then spiral down in a zigzag, wings whistling.

Pick up trail #6 to skirt the southern end of the meadow and you'll soon pass a large, mostly dry kettle hole on the right. This shallow depression was formed by the gradual melting of a block of glacial ice. With the downed maple trees providing a seat upon which to rest, you can gaze upward and perhaps watch a northern oriole building its pendulous nest. The red-eyed vireo calls persistently. Olive green on the back with creamy underparts, its most prominent field mark is its white eyebrow bordered in black. The red eye is visible only at close range. Vireos are notoriously difficult to see, but if you're keen-eyed you may find it.

At the junction here, make a left turn onto trail #3, keeping the meadow on the left. Walking along the meadow's edge is a good way to see birds, which often favor ecotones—the meeting of two different habitats. In this dappled shade, if you are quiet, you are likely to surprise a brown thrasher who has settled on the path to look for something to eat.

The large damp area to the right is another kettle hole, sometimes good for catching a glimpse of the elusive and frustrating yellow-breasted chat. This ventriloquist will drive you crazy as you try to locate it. Easier to spot is the common yellowthroat, a small warbler that resembles the chat. It's olive green on the back and yellow on the underparts, and sports a black face mask, like a bandit.

The kettle hole remains wet much of the year, owing to a heavy clay bottom, and is home to painted turtles, spring peepers, bullfrogs, and wood frogs. Here also are the only native persimmon trees on Long Island. The persimmon tree, which is never very tall and whose trunk rarely exceeds a foot in diameter, has thick, dark brown bark divided into many square plates. The dark green leaves are four to six inches long, wide, leathery, and shiny above. In autumn, when the leaves fall, the egg-shaped fruit is easily seen—at first amber, then becoming orange. Persimmons are too tart to eat until they fall from the tree, but they are a favorite food of bobwhites, flying squirrels, foxes, raccoons, and opossum—all of which live in the preserve.

When trail #3 meets trail #6, switch allegiance and take #6 through the meadow and on up alongside the kame. The kame is a pile of quartz pebbles, chert bits, and sand that's over 220 feet high. A glacial mound—a type of delta—it was built up by a stream that emerged from an ice front that had temporarily stalled. As the front receded, the unsupported back or sides of the accumulation of debris slumped down, leaving a mound. A side path will take you up to the summit. On your way down, note the European larch at the left corner. Not our native larch, which prefers more northern regions, this is an introduced species.

Continue along trail #6 until it meets up with trail #2. Turn left, and follow #2 back to the nature center.

Jones Beach
State Park

Location: Wantagh
Owner: New York State
Distance: up to 3 miles

This is the most famous of all parks on Long Island. It's primarily known as a great beach—which it is—yet few are aware of its rich natural history. Jones Beach is a part of the barrier island that lies between the Atlantic Ocean and various bays (most notably East Bay, South Oyster Bay, and Great Peconic Bay). A state park since 1929, there has been little (if any) development on the island; the stands of pines, tangles of vines, bayberries, and heaths are native. Although recreation facilities have been built, the 2,400-plus acres of Jones Beach State Park are largely in their natural state.

Access

Take Meadowbrook Parkway to its end. After you pass the fee booths, go 1.2 miles to the turnoff for the West End. Turn right here and proceed on Ocean Drive a little over 1 mile to the West End Boat Basin and park in the lot. Public restrooms (not always open in winter) are available.

Although we describe the park in winter, it's a good place to visit year-round. A $4-per car-fee is charged daily from Memorial Day to Labor Day, and on weekends from April 1 to Memorial Day and from Labor Day to Columbus Day.

Trail

As you pull into the West End Boat Basin (also called Short Beach) parking lot on a nice day in January, the first thing you're liable to see out in the boat basin straight ahead of you is a common loon.

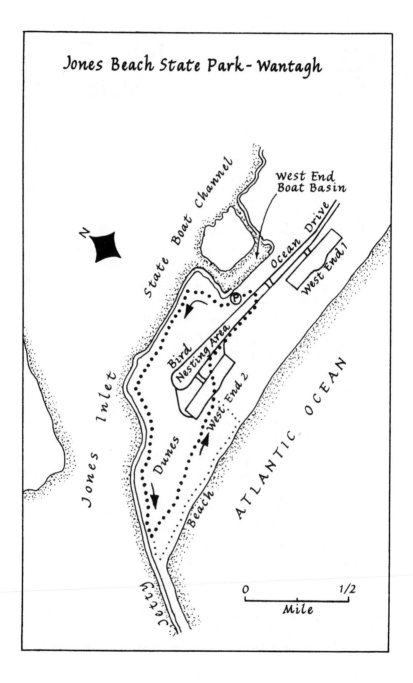

Jones Beach State Park - Wantagh

These big seabirds are often in quite close. Farther out you may spot a horned grebe, diving. Both these seabirds nest in the far north, but find our sheltered bays a fine place to spend the winter.

A great or a double-crested cormorant may be hanging out on a piling. Though similar, they're easy to tell apart: the great (which is here only in winter) has a white belly, and the double-crested will show an orange throat pouch (year-round).

The pines right around the parking lot often host red-breasted nuthatches. You can hear their high, tin-whistle "kng" call. Look for a small bird with a bluish gray back and a rusty breast, climbing head-first down the tree. Nuthatches are so named from their habit of placing nuts (in this case pine seeds gleaned from cones) in the grooves of tree bark to get at the nutmeats.

During fall migration, the lawn here is a good place to find palm warblers, while the pines behind attract other warblers: American redstart, yellow-rumped, and blue-winged. Palms are easy to distinguish—they have rusty caps, yellow breasts, and olive backs, and are found on the ground pumping their tails. The bushes in front of the pines by the Coast Guard station are a good place to look for sparrows and winter finches, such as American goldfinch, pine siskin, dark-eyed junco, American tree sparrow, and fox sparrow. Song sparrows, too, are seen here; they're year-round residents.

In summer, though, the boat basin waters are a haven for common terns. They shriek and dive, ignoring the "No Fishing in this Area" signs. Common terns are difficult to sort out from the similar-looking roseate terns. But look for a bird that is medium gray on the mantle (the roseate is paler) and has a red bill (the roseate's bill is mostly black).

After thoroughly checking the pine stands, head out on a trail that goes left, just before the entrance to the Coast Guard station. This first ¼ mile of the trail will lead you to the edge of Jones Inlet. In summer, the path is lined with wildflowers: white fleabane, Queen Anne's lace, and bladder campion; pink betony, bindweed, and milkweed; goldenrod and butter-and-eggs; and purple deadly nightshade. Closer to the inlet are stands of mullein—tall, yellow, spike-shaped flowers.

Short Beach, east of the boat basin

In the fall, the big rugosa rose bushes are loaded with hips—fleshy, orange fruits that follow the flowers. They are high in nutritional value, and are a favorite food of many birds and mammals.

Year-round you can see large stands of poison ivy, tall phragmites, and bayberry along the track, while the white sand is partly covered by low-growing, dark green heaths.

The inlet is a good place to look for wintering ducks, especially red-breasted merganser and bufflehead. Graceful Bonaparte's gulls—small gulls that fly like terns—coast up and down the inlet, usually on an incoming tide, looking for fish. These winter visitors are much smaller than a herring or black-backed gull, so there's no confusion.

If you continue out to the jetty (a walk of about 1½ miles), do so by following the edge of the inlet. The dunes to the left could harbor a snowy owl—one usually makes an appearance every year or two. Although large (nearly 2 feet tall), because they're white, with a few dark spots, they're surprisingly well camouflaged. Females and young birds have more spots than males, and are therefore easier to see. The snowy is one of the few diurnal owls, which is to say it's active during the day. Snowies are fond of perching on top of a low dune or fence post to watch for prey.

When you get to the jetty, look for northern gannets diving off the tip. These big, cross-shaped, mostly white seabirds are also frequent winter visitors. A somewhat uncommon shorebird that is found here, with some regularity, in late fall and winter is the purple sandpiper. Look for it in the rocks at the base of the jetty. On the shore you should see dunlin and sanderlings, running in and out with the waves, jabbing their bills in the sand as they feed.

The mile-long walk back to West End Field #2 is either through the dunes or along the beach. If you take the dune trail, you might find a wintering eastern meadowlark.

In spring and summer, much of this area is closed off to protect the nesting habitat of least terns and piping plovers—both endangered birds. Black skimmers nest here, too. They're easy to spot: black back, white underparts, and a huge orange bill. They seem to be like terns, and indeed associate with them; but skimmers are a different genus, *Rynchops*—named for their distinctive bills and the way they skim the water's surface to feed.

After you reach the parking lot, take the road back to Short Beach. On the way you should find a small flock of snow buntings and horned larks, both common winter visitors. The snow bunting will be in its winter plumage: white underparts, brownish cap, and brownish back. The horned lark is yellow underneath and brown on the back, with tiny black "horns," really just feathers that stick up over the eyes. Both species are most likely to be encountered on the ground, where they're searching for seeds to eat.

When you drive out of the park, check the dunes. If you're lucky you'll see a short-eared owl hawking—flying low looking for rodents. Although this bird is a resident and breeds in the park, it is most easily found late on winter afternoons.

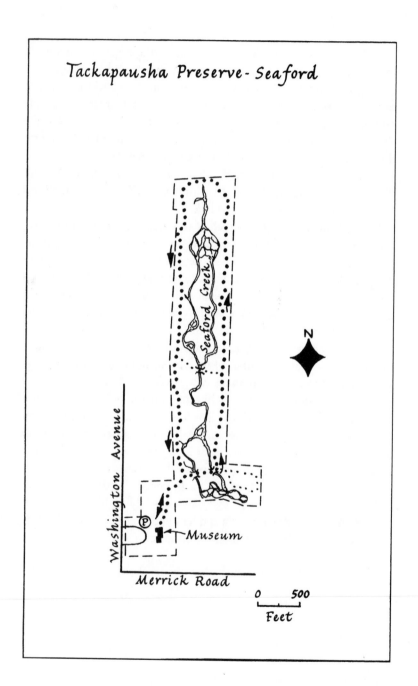

Tackapausha Preserve - Seaford

Washington Avenue

Seaford Creek

Merrick Road

Museum

N

0   500
Feet

Tackapausha Preserve

Location: Seaford
Owner: Nassau County
Distance: 1 mile

Divided into three distinct sections, Tackapausha Preserve is a bit like the housing subdivisions that surround it. The long, narrow slice of land runs from Jerusalem Avenue in the north to Merrick Road in the south, but the preserve is severed once by Clark Street and again by Sunrise Highway. It's as if nature has been allocated its limited space here, to flourish as best it can amid the houses, cars, and highways.

Nevertheless, the preserve amasses to an amazing eighty acres of mostly moist woodland and freshwater marsh. A remnant of the vast glacial outwash plain that makes up the southern half of Long Island, Tackapausha has streams and small ponds in each of its sectors. There's even a snippet of upland woods and a grassy meadow purported to be a mini–Hempstead Plains.

This is not a preserve that lets you forget about civilization; indeed, human beings and their possessions are never far from view or out of earshot. Instead, Tackapausha serves an educational function, helping its neighbors become aware of existing local ecology and what the land was like before their houses were built. What makes Tackapausha truly amazing is its fecundity—its abundance of plants and animals thriving in such a narrow corridor of green. The most interesting walk is in the southern section—twenty acres of very moist woodland dominated by a meandering stream that ultimately drains into the bay farther south.

Access

Take Wantagh State Parkway to exit W6. Then go east on Merrick Road, through the town of Seaford, 1.5 miles to Washington Avenue.

Turn left (north) and go 2 blocks to the preserve; the entrance is on the right.

There are three units to Tackapausha. We discuss the southern section; for information about the central and northern sections, ask at the visitors' center.

Restrooms, a small natural history museum, and a children's gift shop are located in the visitors' center. The preserve is open daylight hours year-round; the visitors' center is open Tuesday through Saturday 10 AM to 4 PM; Sundays 1 PM to 4 PM; closed on Mondays.

Trail

The nature trail begins to the left of the museum building, at the back of the parking lot. You enter an area of "overgrown" lushness—it's weedy and full of vines ambitiously reaching up to the maple limbs drooping overhead. In late summer, the sound of cicadas can be deafening. Whereas in spring and early summer the woods are full of birdsong, by August the insects take the lead role.

Cicadas are large flying insects. Our local dogday harvestfly measures about 1½ inches long, with large, thin, green wings. They are periodical, but not the legendary seventeen-year cicadas. Dogday harvestflies take three years to reach adulthood, and a new generation of nymphs hatches each year. They seem all eyes and wings; the male makes its sawing sound via a special organ below the abdomen. It's our experience that the earlier the cicadas start "buzzing" in the morning, the hotter a day it will be.

The trail soon leads to a little footbridge over Seaford Creek, the first of many times to look down and enjoy the forget-me-nots blooming at streamside. True forget-me-not—in contrast to the garden plant—is a delicate, sprawling plant that loves moisture. Its tiny, light blue flowers have golden eyes that always seem welcoming. Other good things come in small packages, too. Look along the stream for water starwort, a kind of chickweed. This is another low-growing plant that likes to keep its feet wet. Its five small white petals are deeply cleft, or indented. Starwort blooms for much of the year.

Continue on the path directly ahead, then follow it to the left at the T-intersection of trails #1 and #5. The predominant shrub here

Seaford Creek

is clethra, also known as sweet pepperbush because of its pepperlike seeds, growing along with royal and other ferns. Cherry saplings, sassafras, greenbrier, wineberry, and roses provide perches and food for the local birdlife: red-bellied woodpeckers, catbirds, tufted titmice, chickadees, house sparrows. Follow the trail, which parallels the stream, and walk along just inside the preserve fence. Swamp azalea perfumes the air most of the summer. Tupelo and beech trees are interspersed among the lovely, very tall maples.

At various spots along the trail are short paths that lead inward to the stream. Take a few of these and notice the dark and light green patterns of velvet moss. How springy the soil is. At your foot are also likely to be Canada mayflower and Solomon's seal. In contrast to false Solomon's seal, which has its flowers gathered at the tip of its stems, the true plant has flowers that hang like twin bells from each leaf bract along its stems. Some of the joints along the plant's thick rootstock resemble the mark of a seal, hence its name. The ancient Greeks used the roots to close up fresh wounds; they also drank a concoction made from the roots to speed the mending of broken bones. The young shoots of Solomon's seal are edible, used in soups and stews or steamed like asparagus. (But don't pick any here; remember, this is a nature preserve.)

Return to the main path and continue ahead to a fork. Bear right, with the phragmites marsh on the left. There will be an ever-so-slight rise in elevation as you leave the wet woods for a bit higher ground and loop around to the left near the north end of the preserve. At the bend, note the two scarlet oaks growing together and the downed locust tree stretching across the stream. A flicker might fly in front of you; its white rump is a prominent feature of this large woodpecker.

Overhead on this higher ground will be large oak trees (sometimes with Indian pipes growing at their bases) and some American chestnut saplings. A small stand of white pines offers a softness underfoot. The houses nearby indicate the source of the invading plants: yew, barberry, English ivy, wisteria, lily-of-the-valley, pachysandra. In the trees are birds likely to visit both back yard and woodland: cardinal, robin, catbird, tufted titmouse, and chickadee.

The orange trumpet flowers of jewelweed, or spotted touch-me-not, that grow along the path are unmistakable. Jewelweed is a cousin of the garden impatiens; like impatiens, it grows lush in shady spots until frost kills it each fall. Hummingbirds are said to visit jewelweed, although we haven't seen any doing so. Also, people say that sap from the stems will relieve the itching of poison ivy and athlete's foot.

As you approach the other side of the phragmites marsh, you're likely to hear red-winged blackbirds "chucking" and see them clinging to the reed tops. A little farther along, as you again return to the moist woods and pass closer to the stream, will be clumps of false Solomon's seal, yellow flags, and grasses that are favored by birds. A skipper, or perhaps an American copper—two small butterflies in our area—may flit about or alight on a plant. Skippers are a mix of butterfly and moth; they have stocky bodies and large heads; at rest, they keep their forewings open at a 45-degree angle and back wings horizontal. Coppers are reddish or brown and have a coppery luster; the American copper has forewings of copper color spotted with black as well as brown margins.

Follow the trail back to the parking lot, and visit the museum if you wish. Its displays show the geological development of the outwash plain on which Tackapausha resides. In addition, there are exhibits of wetlands ecology, local fish and turtles, trees of the area, and bees, insects, and butterflies. Some live exhibits include the southern leopard frog and northern water snake. The children's gift shop is well stocked with naturalist materials.

Western and Central Suffolk

Woodland fern

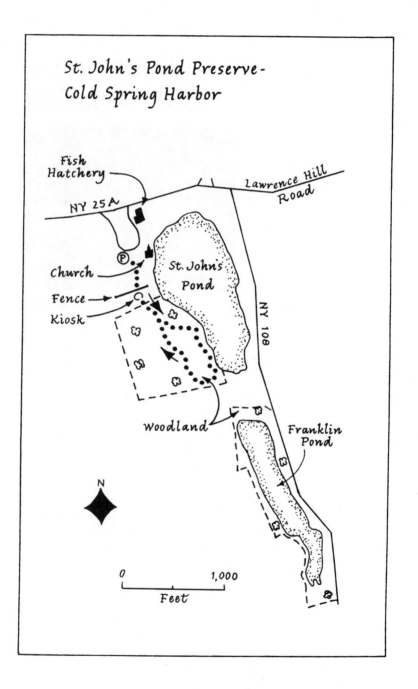

St. John's Pond Preserve-
Cold Spring Harbor

Fish Hatchery

Lawrence Hill Road

NY 25A

St. John's Pond

Church

Fence

Kiosk

NY 108

Woodland

Franklin Pond

N

0   1,000

Feet

St. John's Pond Preserve

Location: Cold Spring Harbor
Owner: The Nature Conservancy
Distance: ¾ mile

I t is May, and high in a treetop a blackburnian warbler sings to proclaim his territory; his throat is flame orange. Down near the pond's edge, northern (Baltimore) orioles weave their intricate, pendulous nests, which hang from high branches. On the forest floor tiny trailing arbutus (also known as ground laurel) sprout their fragrant, pink flowers. Spring is a busy time at St. John's.

Access

St. John's is located adjacent to the state fish hatchery on NY 25A (Northern Boulevard), 0.1 mile west of the intersection with NY 108. The preserve is locked, and the key is obtained from the fish hatchery admission booth. Please be sure to lock the gate behind you! The preserve is open daily 10 AM to 4 PM. There are no public facilities.

Trail

The trail runs through a deciduous woodland with a dense understory of mountain laurel. At the information kiosk (trail maps available), you'll notice that the steep hillside is covered with hay-scented ferns. These ferns have sword-shaped blades with very finely cut margins. The blades always turn to face the light, and, when crushed, they're fragrant.

Take the loop down to the left through a red maple lowland and swampy area nearer the pond. Erosion of the slope is a major problem, and walkers are cautioned to remain on the path. Red maples are our most common maple, and are singular in that there is something red on them in all seasons—from their red buds in winter

Jack-in-the-pulpit

to their crimson foliage in fall. Indeed, St. John's is particularly lovely in autumn, when it is ablaze with color.

The twenty-acre pond spans the Nassau-Suffolk county border. Along with Franklin Pond (of similar size), also in the preserve, it was part of a three-pond system built for industry in the seventeenth century. Now the ponds are home to several turtle and frog species, and a wide variety of waterbirds. Herons and egrets inhabit the shoreline, while pied-billed grebes can be seen out in the middle, diving and often remaining underwater for long periods.

Grebes will sink to escape detection, leaving only their heads exposed. The chicks ride on their parents' backs, even when the parents dive. There are also resident families of Canada geese and mute swans. Mute swans are an exotic—that is, nonnative—bird species. Introduced from Europe in the mid-nineteenth century, the mute swan has been very successful in the Northeast. Although often hand-fed, swans can be aggressive and dangerous, particularly at the nest. In late spring and early summer, the cygnets (baby swans) can be seen hitching rides on the backs of their parents.

The trail continues back through the woodland—chestnut oak, northern red oak, sweet birch, and tulip trees. The tulip tree is in the magnolia family, well known for splendid floral displays. In spring, look for the tulip-shaped flowers for which this tree was named.

Farther along the upland part of the trail, you'll see a large chestnut oak that has had the soil around its roots eroded away. To protect its root system, the tree grew bark over the exposed areas, giving the tree its unusual, gnarled appearance.

Some of the smaller trees you see in this area are American chestnut. Once a proud, tall tree, and among the most valuable of our hardwoods, the American chestnut has been virtually destroyed by chestnut blight, an introduced fungus that attacks the bark. As a result, the trees here are small; they succumb to blight before reaching maturity.

Much of the understory is mountain laurel, which blooms in late May. Canada mayflower, pink lady's slipper, nodding trillium, and trailing arbutus all grow at St. John's. Nodding trillium is one of our favorites; it stands taller than a purple trillium (also found here) and is sweet smelling. Its three leaves can look like a jack-in-the-pulpit (seen here, too), but underneath the leaves hangs its delicate white flower—much the same way that mayapple blossoms hang. The trailing arbutus is another beauty. Its tiny (½-inch) flower is whitish pink. Arbutus—a member of the heath family—grows close to the ground, in among the mosses; as you bend down to smell it you can feel the moss all springy between your fingers, the damp ground at your cheek.

Other wildflowers that you might encounter at St. John's include Solomon's seal, wild geranium, trout lily, and yellow celandine. Native Americans used to use the juice of the celandine to make yellow paints and dyes. The mucky areas near the pond are filled with skunk cabbage and cinnamon ferns. A wide variety of mosses, fungi, and lichens grow on the fallen trees.

Despite three centuries of human activity, there are a number of animals at St. John's. Muskrats and turtles inhabit the marsh, while rabbits, chipmunks, red fox, and opossum live in the woods. Southern flying squirrel, a nocturnal mammal, is also resident. And on summer nights you can hear the whinny of the eastern screech owl. For an exhilarating walk (especially in spring), there is hardly a place better suited than St. John's Pond Preserve.

Uplands Farm Sanctuary

Location: Cold Spring Harbor
Owner: The Nature Conservancy
Distance: ½ mile

U plands Farm is a former dairy and sheep farm, and has served as headquarters for the Long Island chapter of The Nature Conservancy since 1971. During office hours, visitors can obtain information about the Conservancy and use the library. The chapter also sponsors field trips, and holds an annual fair at the farm. Uplands comprises nearly a hundred acres of open fields and woodlands; a section of the Greenbelt Trail crosses the western part of the sanctuary.

Access

From the intersection of NY 110 and NY 25A (Main Street) in Huntington, go west on Main Street to the end of the business district. At the light, where NY 25A branches right, take the left onto Lawrence Hill Road. Proceed 1.5 miles to the entrance (on the left). Come all the way down the driveway, and park to the left of the buildings, by the silo.

The visitors' center, in the recently renovated barn, houses natural history displays and public restrooms.

Trail

The trail starts at the kiosk just beyond the parking lot. It is mostly flat, and is an easy hike. Walkers first travel north, along a hedgerow paralleling an open field. Now that cattle no longer graze here, the field is mowed annually, and timothy and orchard grasses, as well as lots of wildflowers, flourish. The bordering hedgerow is of hickory, oak, and other deciduous trees. Ring-necked pheasants and northern

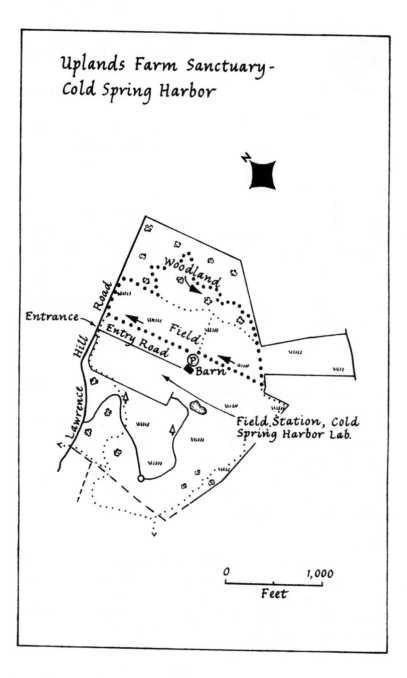

Uplands Farm Sanctuary-
Cold Spring Harbor

bobwhites make the hedgerows their homes as they did a hundred years ago.

Small mammals—eastern cottontail rabbit, white-footed mouse, meadow vole, and shorttail shrew—live in the open fields and brambles. Shrews are mouse-sized, energetic animals that feed on insects, worms, and snails. The shorttail is lead gray with a very short tail; its eyes are so tiny you can scarcely see them. Although common, shrews are not often seen; but you may have them in your yard, as we do.

As you walk along the field you're likely to hear a shrill "killy, killy, killy." That's the call of the American kestrel, our smallest falcon. Kestrels are identified by their rusty back and tail. They hover over open fields, capturing their prey on the ground. Their diet is usually composed of large insects and small reptiles and animals, but in winter they feed on small birds.

After you cross the field, you make your way to the woodland. The place where the field and woods meet is called an ecotone. Ecotones are always rich in plant and animal diversity. Invasive plants, such as the staghorn sumac, with its antlerlike twigs and red fruit clusters, thrive in ecotones. Sumac played a part in early American life. A cooling, lemonade-like drink was made from its fruits, and its leaves and twigs were used in tanning.

This is a second-growth forest, full of oak, beech, and hickory. Arrowwood, one of our native viburnums, produces its showy white blooms in June. In summer, the treelike shrubs are laden with slate blue berries. American robins are fond of feeding on these fruits. Since food has become more available to them, some robins now stay around all year.

The trail loops around before heading back to the field and its hedgerows and thickets. The thickets—consisting mostly of greenbrier, Virginia creeper, and wineberry—provide shelter and food for a number of birds such as gray catbird, black-capped chickadee, red-winged blackbird, indigo bunting, and chipping sparrow. Indigo buntings are small (4½-inch), deep blue birds, with brownish wings. Their long and varied song is especially conspicuous at midday, long after other birdsong has ceased. Chipping sparrows are identified by their bright red caps, white eyebrows, and unstreaked breasts. Their

Winter botany walk

song is a trill of high "chip" notes. In winter, the similar-looking American tree sparrow can be found at the preserve. The tree sparrow has a dark central breast spot and lacks the chipping sparrow's white eyebrow.

As you return to the barn you'll probably notice a flock of house sparrows. Introduced from Europe in the mid-nineteenth century, house sparrows have become ubiquitous. They've been tremendously successful, and, by competing for food and nest sites, have unfortunately pushed out some of our native songbirds.

Around the buildings are sweetgum trees, known by their star-shaped leaves, which in fall turn a brilliant red and gold. Their fruit is a woody, spiny ball, about an inch in diameter. Some of these balls remain on the tree after the leaves have fallen, making the sweetgum an easy tree to identify. There are many species of trees at Uplands, and it is a great place to explore winter botany. Without leaves, you use other clues—such as leaf scar shapes, pith patterns, and twig shapes—to identify trees. It's fun and easy to do here. Uplands is a place to explore nature year-round.

Caumsett State Park

Location: Lloyd Neck
Owner: New York State
Distance: 3 miles

The gracious, curving driveway leads you up into the park from West Neck Road. Soon the stables, barns, and dairy farm buildings come into view. You park near a tall beech tree, set in a meadow that ripples before you like a huge green blanket. Birds call from the nearby woodland: orioles, cardinals, robins, chickadees, titmice, nuthatches. A pair of house sparrows are busy building a nest in one of the barns.

This was once the Marshall Field estate. Field called it by its original Matinecock Indian name, Caumsett, meaning "place by a sharp rock." Situated on a scenic peninsula that juts out into Long Island Sound, the park comprises meadows, woodland, salt marsh, and a rocky shore.

The rocky shore of the park continues to the east, to Target Rock National Wildlife Refuge, another former estate. The fourteen-foot-high rock for which the refuge is named stands a short distance from the shoreline. British soldiers reportedly used it for target practice during the Revolutionary War. At that time the rock was embedded in the bluff, long since eroded away. The wildlife and terrain of Target Rock are similar to that of Caumsett.

Access

From the intersection of West Neck Road and NY 25A (Main Street) in Huntington, go north on West Neck Road approximately 5 miles until you reach the park entrance (on the left).

The park is open daily from 8 AM to 4:30 PM. A $3 fee (per car) is charged daily from Memorial Day weekend through Labor Day

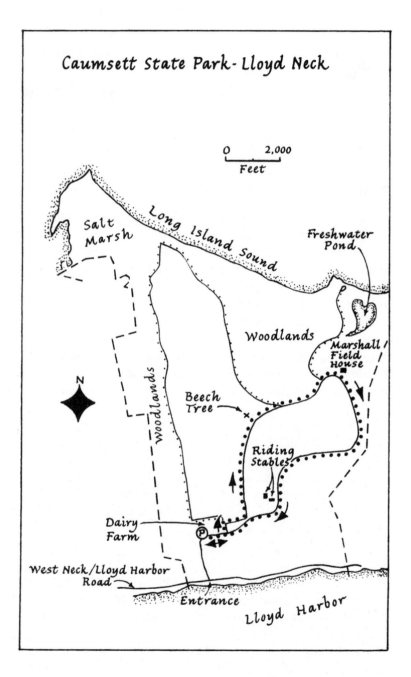

Caumsett State Park- Lloyd Neck

Swallowtail butterfly

weekend and on weekends from April 1 to Memorial Day and from Labor Day to Columbus Day. At other times admission is free. Public restrooms are located both at the Dairy Farm (near the entrance) and at the Marshall Field house; there are no other facilities. For information about guided walks, interpretive tours, and educational programs, call 516-423-1770.

The 3-mile loop to and from the Marshall Field house is entirely paved and wheelchair accessible. Although we describe this loop, there is a vast network of trails throughout the park's 1,500 acres and visiting all its habitats.

Volunteers for Wildlife, a wildlife rehabilitation center, is located at the Dairy Farm. Queens College Center for Environmental Teaching and Research has its headquarters in the Marshall Field house.

Trail

After passing the dairy farm complex, the trail leads across a meadow toward the riding stables. This is a good area for field birds, and we've seen yellow warbler, common yellowthroat, palm warbler, red-winged blackbird, field sparrow, European starling, northern cardinal, and brown-headed cowbirds here. One year we were lucky enough to come upon a small flock of bobolinks, as they passed through on spring migration. These gorgeous black birds sport silver wings and a golden nape. They breed in tall-grass prairies or flooded meadows, and have lost most of their breeding range in the East, owing to early cutting of hayfields.

Soon you're in an open woodland, mostly dogwood, with an understory of wood geranium: white and pink and green. Narcissus have naturalized here and bloom in May, right along with the wood geraniums. Also in bloom are wood hyacinths, which look like bluebells. This gently wooded area is a great place to see migrating warblers: black-and-white, yellow-rumped (myrtle), blue-winged. Perhaps you'll catch a glimpse of an American redstart flashing its orange wing patches as it catches flies. Or see the brilliant orange throat of the blackburnian warbler. Often scarlet tanagers flit through the woodland. They nest at Caumsett, bringing a bit of the tropics to us Long Islanders.

About a mile in, on the left, is a huge beech tree set in the middle of a meadow. Although lovely at any season, it's a knockout in its fall colors. And on the other side of the path are wildflowers: jack-in-the-pulpit, lady's thumbprint, Solomon's seal, false Solomon's seal, violets, and more wood geranium. Branching off the main track are bridle paths. These are narrower, but open to the adventurous walker. You won't see as many birds, but you may find more wildflowers. The one off to the right just beyond the big beech tree has had nesting northern (Baltimore) orioles. These large orange-and-black songsters are frequent breeders at Caumsett. They weave a pendulous nest of plant fiber strips and line it with fine grasses, plant down, and hair. But they *weave* it—without hands!

As the poet May Swenson wrote, "feel like A Bird / understand / he has no hand / instead A Wing / close-lapped / mysterious thing. . . ."

Soon you'll come to the house. As you approach it, the path is bordered by rhododendrons on one side, lawn on the other. Look here for bank swallows. These cliff-dwelling birds nest in the bluffs at Caumsett and neighboring Target Rock. Also around the house you should see chipping sparrows with their jaunty red caps and white eyelines. They love the tall conifers here, as do American goldfinches. Behind the manor house, Queens College has some large birds in cages. These are for educational purposes, but you may visit them and get a close-up look at a barred owl, a pair of bald eagles, and various young hawks, including a way-out-of-range Harris's hawk. (Harris's hawks are resident in the Southwest, and no one is sure how this one got here. Perhaps it escaped from a falconer's collection.)

Continue on the road past the house through the woodland and back to the riding stables. Many of the same birds, trees, and flowers are to be found here. You might hear the ascending "wheep, wheep" call of the great crested flycatcher, a handsome bird with a rusty tail, pale yellow breast, and brownish crest. Or a yellow-billed cuckoo might sail across the road and hide deep in a tree. Cuckoos have long, spotted tails, and are quite large (11-inch) birds, while the flycatcher, for instance, is only 7 inches. Paradoxically, though, the flycatcher will be easier to see because it's active and out in the open, while the cuckoo is a skulker.

The old brick stables stand out against the modern aluminum ones of today. Starlings and house sparrows are frequenters of horse yards. And as you round the bend, you may be greeted by a flock of Canada geese that strut around the lawns between the stables and the parking lot as if they owned the place.

If you want to visit Target Rock, turn left as you exit the park and continue to the end of the road. Just before the entrance to the refuge, you'll pass the largest black oak *(Quercus velutina)* tree in the nation—over twenty-one feet in girth and more than eighty feet tall—famous as one of Long Island's champions.

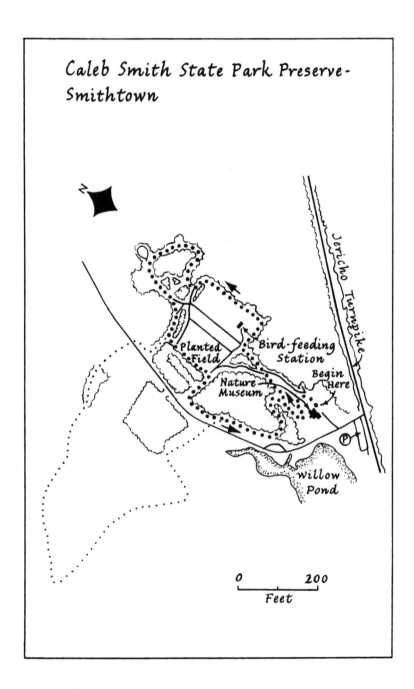

Caleb Smith State Park Preserve-
Smithtown

N

Jericho Turnpike

Planted
Field

Bird-feeding
Station

Begin
Here

Nature
Museum

P

Willow
Pond

0   200
Feet

Caleb Smith
State Park Preserve

Location: Smithtown
Owner: New York State
Distance: 1 mile

Although its neighbors are housing tracts and shopping malls, Caleb Smith State Park Preserve embraces a portion of what was once untamed Long Island. The virgin Nissequogue River flows through the park much as it did when the Nesaquake Indians owned the land. And the bordering wetlands, fields, and woods support a wide variety of native flora and fauna.

The Nissequogue derives from springs in nearby Blydenburgh County Park and Weld Pond. Its fresh, cool water flows northward, cutting across both terminal moraines, and meanders through Caleb Smith Park. As the river gradually widens and turns brackish, it empties into Long Island Sound.

In 1663, the Smith family (for whom Smithtown is named) leased the land from the Native Americans and began many years of farming. The river was a popular fishing spot, and in 1888 the Brooklyn Gun Club (later renamed the Wyandanch Fish and Game Club) began buying the land and allowing the fields to revert. In 1963, the state purchased the property, and by 1974 it was a state park. To ensure the preservation of its unique environment, the state designated it as a park preserve (limited use), and in 1982 named the Nissequogue a Scenic and Recreational River.

Access

From Sunken Meadow State Parkway, take exit 3 east to Jericho Turnpike (NY 25). Proceed for 3 miles to the park entrance, on the left. A permit, issued on the spot, is necessary for visiting the preserve; $1 per person is charged. There are public restrooms (wheelchair accessible) located in the museum building. The preserve is open from 8 AM to 4:30 PM Tuesday through Sunday, from April 1 to September 30; the rest of the year it's open Wednesday through Sunday.

An all-access nature trail is a ½-mile loop beginning behind the nature museum and continuing on to Willow Pond.

Fly-fishing (for brown, brook, and rainbow trout) is by reservation only; call 516-265-1054. Trails are marked for cross-country skiing; for permits and trail conditions, also call 516-265-1054.

Trail

Park headquarters are located in the gracious Smith farmhouse, framed by the towering locust trees and set off by a gently sloping lawn. Photographs in the house show the original 1751 structure, which was expanded considerably when the property became the sportsmen's club. Much of the first floor is now a nature museum, with excellent exhibits on local butterflies, fish, reptiles and amphibians, birds, and flowers.

The Yellow Trail begins in back of park headquarters, in the midst of an herb garden. Dug where the Smiths would have grown their herbs, the garden shows the medicinal, textile, and culinary herbs of the eighteenth century. Look for betony, wormwood, comfrey, and motherwort among the medicinal herbs; tansy and southernwood grow with the herbs used for dyeing textiles; while mint, strawberry, hollyhock, lemon balm, chives, and hedge mustard are some of the culinary herbs.

Shortly, you will pass alongside a small meadow. In summer, cabbage white butterflies dance among the flowers. A crop pest, this European species was introduced into the United States a century ago and is now widespread. The sweet, strong scent here is the Japanese honeysuckle, another introduced species and also a pest. You'll find it climbing over every tree and shrub in its path as it shows off its delicate beige and white trumpet flowers.

This small field is a good place to look for wildflowers such as vetch, chicory, buttercup, common milkweed, black-eyed Susan, butterflyweed, daisy fleabane, hyssop-leaved boneset, sweet everlasting, daisy, yellow hawkweed, and mullein. Check here also for song spar-

Willow Pond

rows, whose dark center breast spot makes them easy to identify among other birds. They often sing from a conspicuous perch.

As you follow the trail into the woods, you'll pass wineberry and raspberry bushes as well as wild grape and wild roses. The flowering roses scent the air. These thickets are favorites of catbirds and cardinals, which often sing while hidden among the branches. The trees around you are mostly oaks, locust, and black cherry.

With its dark red-brown bark, the black cherry has a smooth-grained wood that is highly valued for furniture, while its fruit is used in cough medicines and sometimes to flavor brandy. Cherry trees are often easy to spot because of the large, knobby galls that grow on their trunks and branches; this is black knot, a common fungus.

In the woods, look for Canada mayflower, false Solomon's seal, nodding trillium, sessile bellwort, wood anemone, Indian pipe, and turk's-cap lily. False Solomon's seal is easily distinguished from Solomon's seal: the flowers of the true plant occur in pairs at each leaf base, while the false plant has the flowers only at the tip of the stem. Indian pipe is a white, waxy plant of a single stem topped with a single white flower. The plant gets its nourishment from decayed material in tree roots. In the trees are likely to be chickadees and titmice, white-breasted nuthatches, and red-bellied woodpeckers, while a veery, robin, or wood thrush might be hopping along the ground or perched on a low branch.

The trail makes a sharp right turn to follow along the side of a reverting field. Check the bird-feeding station for sparrows and finches. Also, the meadow is an active area for wildlife, even though much of it goes undetected. The honeysuckle-covered eastern redcedars provide cover for cardinals and mockingbirds, while goldenrod, wild carrot (Queen Anne's lace), yarrow, and milkweed attract bees and butterflies. Tunneling among the roots of these plants are meadow mice, voles, shrews, and moles. Indeed, the extent of activity below the surface of a meadow is extraordinary. And flitting above the flowers are dragonflies and damselflies.

As you stroll along, listen for the "bob-bob-WHITE" of the northern bobwhite, a chunky, reddish brown quail with a gray tail. The bobwhite builds its nest on the ground, usually in tall grass tangled with vines. The young leave the nest almost as soon as they hatch, scurrying along with their parents when disturbed. By the way, the bobwhite feeds on the berries of the Japanese honeysuckle, that vigorous, introduced vine mentioned earlier.

Soon the trail curves back into the woods, passing by eastern redcedars, oaks, red maples, and lots of poison ivy. Careful! Poison ivy is a valuable wildlife plant—its berries are rich food for many birds—but brushing up against even a little bit can bring a maddeningly itchy rash. Along here we have found box turtles, a common resident on Long Island. Actually a tortoise, the box turtle may well live up to 150 years, perhaps because of its ability to draw up its undershell and completely "box" itself in as protection.

As you follow the edge of a field you'll see that, instead of meadow flowers, here are planted tall stands of millet, corn, sunflowers, oats, and buckwheat. These crops are grown as feed for animals, especially birds. Red-winged blackbirds and grackles can't wait for the seed to be put in the feeders—they're in the field helping themselves.

When you begin to pass through the wetter area, you are nearing the river and the vegetation changes somewhat. Here are mosses and ferns, skunk cabbage, red maples, and spicebush. A deciduous shrub with dense clusters of tiny yellow flowers in spring, the spicebush is often called the "forsythia of the wild." Its bark is used medicinally and its fruit is dried and used as a spice.

In spring, this wet area becomes a vernal pond, a breeding spot for tree frogs, salamanders, and spring peepers. The wildflowers that are apt to be here are marsh blue violet and spotted touch-me-not. You're likely to hear the "witchity-witchity" of the common yellowthroat, a yellow-and-olive warbler with a black face mask.

As you approach Willow Pond, look for northern orioles, which like to build their pendulous grassy nests near water. Especially for young anglers, the pond is stocked with trout, bluegill, pumpkinseed, and largemouth bass. The cold, spring-fed water also permits brook, brown, and rainbow trout to survive here. Water plants growing along the shore include water starwort and water milfoil. Green frogs often leap into the water upon your approach.

When you return to the parking lot, check the purple martin houses on the side of park headquarters. These large, dark swallows nest colonially, but often the houses that are put up for them are taken over by house sparrows.

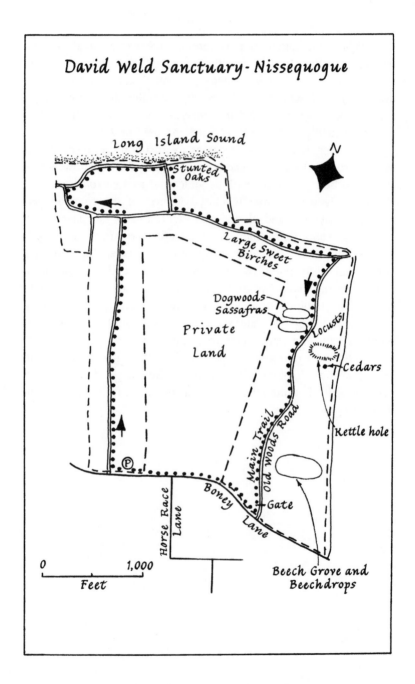

David Weld Sanctuary - Nissequogue

Long Island Sound

N

Stunted Oaks

Large Sweet Birches

Dogwoods Sassafras

Locusts

Private Land

Cedars

Kettle hole

Main Trail

Old Woods Road

P

Horse Race Lane

Boney Lane

Gate

0   1,000

Feet

Beech Grove and Beechdrops

David Weld Sanctuary

Location: Nissequogue (Smithtown)
Owner: The Nature Conservancy
Distance: 2 miles

Open fields, transitional and climax woodlands, and a magnificent fifty-foot bluff overlooking Long Island Sound are all part of the David Weld Sanctuary. The bluff offers unsurpassed vistas. It's no wonder that there was a small cottage here at one time. Called the "Watchman's Cabin," it was built in the 1930s by Cornelia Otis Skinner. She chose the spot so that she'd have a peaceful place to write and rehearse. And what writer wouldn't appreciate such a setting! The first time we visited here, in the early 1970s, we saw the cabin, all boarded up, and wondered about it. Only stories now remain.

Access

From NY 25A (North Country Road), turn right at the top of the hill west of Smithtown onto Edgewood Avenue. After 1 mile, turn left onto Nissequogue River Road. Go 3 miles to the end and turn left onto Horse Race Lane. Go 0.5 mile to a grassy triangle with trees and turn left onto Boney Lane. The entrance is 0.2 mile on the right. There is a parking lot and an information kiosk.

Trail

The David Weld Sanctuary lies at the mouth of the Nissequogue River—the only river on Long Island that flows north. This 124-acre preserve was a gift of David and Mollie Weld. Gifts are in large part the way The Nature Conservancy acquires land.

The preserve is shaped like an inverted U, and the trail begins along an old road through reverting fields, north toward Long Island

Tree mushroom

Sound. Here the perfume from the rampant wild roses permeates the air. Yellow warblers flit about, and red-winged blackbirds call their "ko-churree" from the tops of tangles. As soon as you get to the woodland, the piercing whistle of northern bobwhites takes over. "Bob-bob-WHITE! Bob-bob-WHITE!" A small covey of them scurries along the ridge and disappears into the understory.

At the fork (about ½ mile from the trailhead), bear left and you will soon come to a bluff overlooking Long Island Sound. In winter this is a good place to look for sea ducks. We've seen common goldeneye, bufflehead, long-tailed duck (oldsquaw), and white-winged scoter as they bob up and down in the waves, diving for fish.

In spring and summer the bluff is dotted with the nest holes of bank swallows. You can stand here and watch them dart in and out, bringing in nesting material—grass, rootlets, and feathers. Their burrows are two to three feet deep, and though they usually excavate them themselves, they sometimes will use a deserted kingfisher burrow. Bank swallows nest in colonies, and this one comprises about thirty pairs. Two weeks or so after eggs are laid the chicks hatch—helpless, blind, and naked. But in only three weeks they fledge. Virtually insectivorous, bank swallows catch their prey on the wing, and while they're feeding young, they can be seen making many, many trips to and from their nest holes.

On an offshore rock, double-crested cormorants dry out their wings. Cormorants are black and bronze fish-eating birds that dive from the surface and swim underwater. Their eyes are adapted for aerial as well as underwater vision, because the eye muscles can alter the shape of the lens. This gives them the keenest underwater vision of any animal.

Follow the trail as it turns right, through a "forest" of stunted oak trees. At a T-intersection, turn left. Here you are amid large sweet birches. Their twigs have a strong wintergreen flavor. The sweet birch's bark is reddish brown, marked with horizontal slashes; it doesn't peel the way a paper birch's does.

Passing by private lands on the left, the trail narrows considerably as it leads through a mixed woodland: dogwood, sassafras, locust, eastern redcedar. Two huge kettle holes here are remnants from eons gone by when Long Island was covered by a glacier. The woody vines and thickets that grow throughout the preserve make ideal nesting and feeding spots for birds. Among the species seen here are Carolina wren, gray catbird, northern mockingbird, red-eyed vireo, blue-winged warbler, yellow-breasted chat, and northern cardinal.

The chat is a large (6½- to 7½-inch) warbler with a yellow breast and an olive green back; it has a black facial mask with white "spectacles." An accomplished ventriloquist, the chat's calls are so varied that at times you wonder if all that you're hearing is coming from a single bird. Although classified as a wood warbler, the yellow-breasted chat has many unwarbler-like characteristics, such as its thick bill and its habit of holding food (insects and berries) with its foot.

As you approach the gate, you pass through a grove of American beech trees. Beechdrops, a parasitic wildflower, grow here as well. The flowers parasitize the tree roots, and so are found right around the trunks. Look for brownish tan stems, six to eighteen inches high. From August to October you may see the white and magenta tubular flowers, but at any season you should be able to see the dried stalks.

Farther on is a remarkable stand of pink lady's slipper—nearly a hundred plants—remarkable because half of them are white. This is a rare albino form. Other wildflowers that proliferate here are jack-in-the-pulpit, spotted wintergreen, Canada mayflower, spring beauty, and Indian pipe. Wild leek—known to us as ramps—also grow here. There is lots and lots of poison ivy, so be careful.

When you get to the gate, just continue on to the road (Boney Lane), turn right, and walk ½ mile back to the parking area.

Connetquot River State Park Preserve

Location: Oakdale
Owner: New York State
Distance: 2½ miles

People don't usually think of Long Island in terms of its rivers, even though we have several quite respectable ones on this whale-shaped island. The Connetquot begins in the north of the park, where springs gush clear, cool water year-round. The water flows over a bed of sand and glacial pebbles toward the river's mouth at Great River. But on its way it cuts a path through some of the loveliest woodland on the South Shore. Here, where the river supports trout and other aquatic species that demand pristine water, you will also see herons, egrets, ducks, swans, and osprey. Connetquot is also an excellent place to catch a look at deer in the wild, as well as wild turkeys. And, of course, the woods have nesting ring-necked pheasant, ruffed grouse, northern bobwhite, American woodcock, eastern screech-owl, great horned owl, several woodpecker species, and many song-birds, including eastern bluebird, our state bird.

Access

The park is on Sunrise Highway, 1.5 miles east of exit 44 off the Southern State Parkway. Because the park is on the north side of the highway, it is necessary (if you approach from the west) to continue 0.3 mile past the entrance and make a U-turn. *A permit (free) is required to visit the park, and must be obtained in advance.* Write a brief letter to Connetquot River State Park Preserve, PO Box 505, Oakdale, NY 11769. Give your name and address, what you wish to do in the preserve, and how many people will accompany you. You may call 516-581-2100 for further information. An entrance fee of $1 per person is charged. The park is closed on Mondays.

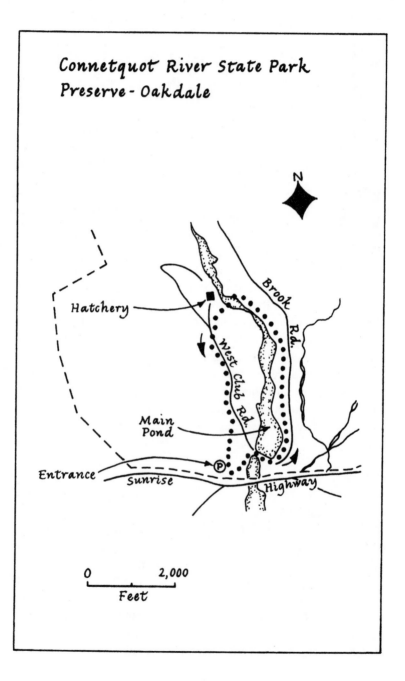

Connetquot River State Park Preserve - Oakdale

N

Hatchery

Brook Rd.

West Club Rd.

Main Pond

Entrance

Sunrise

Highway

P

0   2,000
        Feet

Restrooms are located in the administration building, a short distance from the parking lot, and also at the fish hatchery. Fly-fishing, horseback riding, and cross-country skiing opportunities are offered at the park, and guided walks and interpretive tours (2-hour, 2-mile walks) are presented during the season. Contact the preserve office (516-581-1005) for reservations and information.

Many of the trails are wheelchair accessible, including West Club Road, which runs for a mile from the entrance to the fish hatchery. Although the trails we've described here (Red and Yellow) when taken together are about 2½ miles long, there are several other trails, including the 8½-mile Blue Trail, which traverses the length of the park.

Trail

With almost 3,475 acres, Connetquot River State Park Preserve is a world unto itself. Once the property of the South Side Sportsmen's Club, the park seems like a summer camp in New England, with rustic cedar-shake buildings scattered about the lawn, beneath sprawling white oak trees. One of the buildings is Snedecor's Tavern, built in 1820 and used as a clubhouse by the sportsmen from 1860 to 1973. Around the buildings, look for chipping sparrows on the lawn and barn swallows swooping across the mowed field. Closer to the river is the Oakdale Grist Mill, dating back to 1760. Owned by the Nichols family, the mill ran for a century, grinding cornmeal and wheat flour for local farmers. It also pulled woven cloth and sawed wood.

As you pass the mill, you're likely to see fly-fishers flinging their long yellow fish lines backward and then far into the river below. Fly-fishing (available by reservation) is permitted for brook, brown, and rainbow trout. The brown trout are native to Long Island, but the brook and rainbow are stocked. (The trail goes to the fish hatchery, upriver.)

Follow the Red Trail as it leads through woods consisting largely of maples, with skunk cabbage and ferns filling every available spot of ground. There are also some groupings of jack-in-the-pulpit, especially where the oaks, spicebush, and arrowwood viburnum are growing. Note how saturated the ground is where it borders the

A pair of female turkeys

stream. Along here you're also likely to spot a dark chestnut butterfly with a yellow margin to its wings—the mourning cloak. On the trees are bat boxes—long, slim, down-turned wooden boxes with narrow slats inside. Little brown, big brown, and red bats nest in the park.

In this woodland, dense with vines and thickets, you're apt to encounter birds that enjoy the fruits and tangles of this vegetation: gray catbird, brown thrasher, rufous-sided towhee, hermit and wood thrushes, American robin, northern mockingbird. In spring you may also see some of the wood warblers in migration: northern parula, chestnut-sided, magnolia, Cape May, black-throated blue, blackpoll, and northern waterthrush; in summer, you're more likely to see pine or prairie warblers, or black-and-white warblers and ovenbirds.

As you continue on the Red Trail, you'll soon enter an area of open woodlands, mostly pitch pine and highbush blueberry. Take the short path to the left; it brings you to a fishing platform that juts out into the river just above the pond (platform #8). Go quietly; if you're lucky, you'll see a pair of wood ducks near their nesting box. Watch overhead, too, for an osprey as it flies up and down the river, looking for fish. And check the branches that overhang the river for northern orioles.

Your streamside perch will also be an excellent seat for watching a mute swan attempt to lift off; perhaps the stream acts as a runway. In any event, the grunting bird thump-thump-thumps along, flapping its heavy wings and paddling its pink webbed feet along the water's surface until it is airborne.

Return to the Red Trail and continue along through the blueberries and pines. Watch for the occasional deer's head above the blueberry bushes. The deer feed actively at dusk and dawn, but can also be seen during the day in open areas. Look at the sandy trail; often you'll see deer tracks before you encounter the animals. And at times you'll find clumps of their hair clinging to low branches or tree trunks.

As the trail winds closer to the water again, you're likely to hear the common yellowthroat's "witchity-witchity" song. These little warblers sport jet black masks and bright yellow throats, and are fairly easy to see. They also respond well to "pishing"—a noise birders make to try to get birds to come out into the open. Here, too, you might see a field sparrow—look for its diagnostic pink bill and legs. Overhead, a flash of brilliant red may well be a scarlet tanager; they're common nesters in the park. Black-capped chickadees and white-breasted nuthatches frequently accompany walkers along the trail.

It may be a bit confusing, but follow the Red Trail markers to the fish hatchery (look for great egrets relishing the plentiful supply of fish) and cross over the stream. A black-crowned night heron usually roosts in a nearby tree. Note the water starwort, cattail, and forget-me-not that seek this moist area. (At the hatchery there are benches and toilets, should you need them.)

Now pick up the Yellow Trail. Just as you leave the hatchery you'll walk a stretch of the Greenbelt Trail—a 34-mile north-south trail that crosses the island from Sunken Meadow to Heckscher State Parks. The Yellow Trail goes through an area of mostly pine barrens, which extend from this point eastward toward Southampton. These woods are largely scrub oak and pitch pine. The scrub oak is a nondescript short tree with leathery leaves that grows where many other trees won't. Pitch pines, sometimes called black pines or sap pines, also are short trees, which take on odd forms as the wind and weather shape them. They are knotty and resist decay; after a fire, pitch pines will sprout new growth at their bases. You'll pass a couple of fire breaks that have been cut through the pines; in one such fire break there's a pole with an osprey nest on top.

On the way back to the parking lot, keep your eyes and ears open for wild turkey; they are commonly seen around the buildings. As we came down the path, three females rambled across in front of us. Then we heard a loud gobble, and turned to see a fanned tail emerge from the grass. It was the male turkey and these three were his harem. He called and strutted, shimmering his tail and circling slowly, showing his barred underparts and the high ruffle of black feathers on his back. The females continued toward him, pecking at the occasional seed on the ground, but clearly, he wanted them to follow him to a preferred feeding spot.

The trail concludes at the barn. In the weedy fields between the barn and the parking lot you might spot some butterflies. Look for common buckeye, common wood nymph, and red admiral.

Sunken Forest/Fire Island National Seashore

Location: Sailors Haven
Owner: National Park Service
Distance: 1½ miles

From November 1854 to June 1857, five ships, nine barks, sixteen brigs, twenty-five schooners, and nine sloops were wrecked or in distress off the southern coast of Long Island. A gazetteer from 1860 comments that "the traveler along the beach is seldom out of sight of a wreck." It is said that Fire Island got its name from the beach fires that pirates built at night to lure cargo ships onto the shore. But by 1858, the Fire Island Lighthouse was helping guide ships past the western tip of this 32-mile barrier island, avoiding the sandbars and pirates to reach safe harbor.

The pirates are gone and sand deposited by ocean currents has extended the western point of Fire Island almost five miles beyond the lighthouse. People continue to come to Fire Island, but now it's for the solitude and sunshine. In 1964, Fire Island National Seashore was established to preserve the only developed barrier island in the United States without roads.

Located at Sailors Haven, the Sunken Forest is a lovely walk through a maritime woodland nestled between the sand dunes and a salt marsh.

Access

Take exit 44E off the Southern State Parkway onto Sunrise Highway (NY 27). Go east for 4.5 miles to Lakeland Avenue and turn right (south). Continue for 2 miles to Main Street (in Sayville) and turn left (following the green-and-white "Fire Island Ferry" signs). Take your first right (0.2 mile) onto Foster Avenue to Terry Avenue (0.6 mile), and turn left, then right again after 1 block. Parking for the ferries

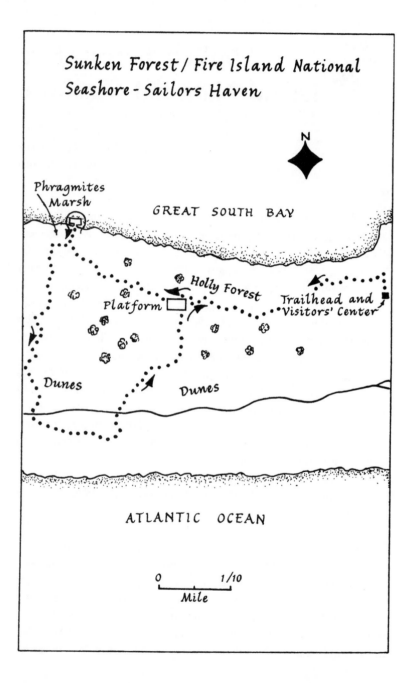

is in a large lot on the right. Parking fees range from $6 to $8, depending on the season.

Take the Sailors Haven Ferry, which runs six times a day in July and August, once (or twice) a day the rest of the year. Call 516-589-8980 for schedules. Round-trip tickets are $8 (adults) and $4.50 (children).

The visitors' center is open daily, 9:30 AM to 5 PM, in summer. The schedule is irregular for the remainder of the year. Near the visitors' center is a small concession stand that sells refreshments; a gift shop and restrooms are located at the concession. Picnic tables are near the marina.

Wheelchair users can take the trail right through the forest, as far as the Great South Bay overlook, after which there are steps. There are some steep, though short, ups and downs on the trail.

Trail

As you walk down the dock from the ferry, you immediately see the visitors' center ahead of you. The trail to the Sunken Forest is to the right. With exhibits on bay fish, ocean shells, and trees of the forest, the visitors' center is worth a stop before you begin the trail.

The trail is boardwalk all the way, and very easy going. Almost instantly you are in the midst of a vegetative tangle—mostly green-brier, wild grape, Virginia creeper, and poison ivy entwining the saplings of black cherry, oak, and maple. The dappled light makes patchwork patterns on the tree trunks, while the persistent "meow" of catbirds sounds from within the thicket. In spring and fall, an American redstart—a species of wood warbler—may pause in its migration to pick insects from among the berries and blossoms, flashing its twin orange or yellow tail patches.

Although it appears to be in a depression, the Sunken Forest is not truly "sunken." The ocean winds pick up grains of sand and deposit them on the dune, building an embankment behind which these trees prosper. Also, the constancy of the sea breezes keeps the treetops pruned to no higher than the dune. At times these woods seem tropical, they are so humid and still. How dark and quiet it is, compared to the bright, roaring beach beyond!

The dominant tree of the forest is the American holly. Easily recognized by their dark green, prickly leaves, the holly trees here are estimated to be at least 200 years old. The thick, smooth, light gray trunks turn and twist in lovely shapes, and are host to lichens that add pleasing colors and patterns. We know the holly as a small tree or shrub, whose red-berried boughs are used at Christmas to decorate our hearths. The name is probably a corruption of the world *holy,* although there is evidence of its indoor use in pagan times. American holly is particularly a species of southern regions—indeed, it was a favorite of George Washington, who grew several at Mount Vernon—but the moderating influence of the Gulf Stream has ensured its place here.

The holly marks this as a climax forest—a mature woodland that will not be supplanted unless a storm, or other disaster, drastically alters the environment. Another tree that is indicative of a climax forest is the sassafras. You'll see it growing intermittently among the hollies. Look for its rich red bark—like a chocolate velvet cake. This aromatic tree is noted botanically for its variations in leaf form, the most recognizable of which is the "mitten" shape that appears on new growth. Although sassafras can grow up to eighty feet high and have a trunk six feet thick in the South, we have much smaller specimens in the Northeast.

The sassafras has a checkered history. The roots yield an oil that was used by Native Americans for its aromatic properties, but early explorers brought back claims far greater. Demands in Europe for sassafras grew tremendously, as it was seen as a curative at a time when no one understood very much about illness. Sassafras was one of the first exports sent by Captain John Smith from the Jamestown colony. But the public soon lost faith in sassafras, relegating it to a "spring tonic" and then to just a tea.

As you pass through the forest, you're sure also to see the twisted, streaky clumps of the shadblow, also called shadbush or juneberry or serviceberry. Why does the tree have many different names? Sometimes growing as a tree and sometimes as a shrub, the shadblow bursts with dainty white flowers in early spring, when the shad run. In June, its purple berries are food for robins and mockingbirds. The small round leaves in autumn turn a lovely yellow. This native tree grows

The boardwalk through a grove of shadbush and holly trees

throughout the eastern United States, but takes on fanciful shapes in the Sunken Forest.

The leaf litter on the forest floor covers the sandy ground so well that you might think you're in a moist, nutrient-rich woodland. American robins perch on downed limbs, and rufous-sided towhees scratch for insects and seeds on the ground. The scene is a mosaic of leaf colors and shapes. There is much green growth here, but the soil is not rich in nutrients. In fact, the leaf cover is very thin, and below

114 · *Walks and Rambles on Long Island*

it is but six inches of humus. The roots of most of these plants penetrate no farther than this humus layer, as can be seen when you pass an upturned tree.

As you approach a large, planked area (where intepretative programs are sometimes given), continue straight ahead, farther along the trail through the forest. In places, you're likely to see small pools of standing water or muddy spots. Just how wet the ground is—and consequently how present the mosquitoes are—is a reflection of both the amount of precipitation and the height of the tides. A lens of fresh water floats atop the salt water in the ground, and when tides are running high, the freshwater layer is buoyed up, making the forest damper than normal.

Look here for signs of resident red fox, cottontail rabbit, longtail weasel, and mice. Also evident might be hognose snake, black racer, or Fowlers toad. Whitetail deer, whose populations have been increasing on Long Island for decades, are now a frequent sight in the forest. Look for the bushy, wedge-shaped tail, which is snowy white underneath and on the edges. When alarmed and running away, the whitetail deer holds its tail erect in a conspicuous manner—seemingly in defiance of laws of protective coloration among animals.

The tupelo, or sour gum, trees also indicate a boggy area. In the standing water are groupings of cattails and phragmites, whereas less saturated areas are hosts to ferns. The swamp fleabane points its flowers of pink cups skyward. A mourning cloak butterfly, its velvety brown wings looking like a funeral shawl, skips with joy among the greens. A Carolina wren calls its "tea-kettle, tea-kettle" for all to hear.

At the intersection, follow the trail out to Great South Bay. The adjacent thickets are largely groundsel, a weedy shrub that favors coastal wetlands; its greenish white flowers burst open in August and September. Herring gulls and a solitary sandpiper patrol the beach for food, while tree swallows catch their meals in midair. At the shore, notice the thick mat of eelgrass at the high tide line—it's about a foot thick and three to four feet wide. A flowering marine grass, it grows underwater and provides food for innumerable fish and waterbirds, especially brant, a small, dark goose. Eelgrass also provides shelter for shellfish, most notably scallops.

Return to the main trail and continue around the marsh, passing through more of the Sunken Forest. You then climb the dune and overlook the swale to the next dune. The swale is the valley of fresh air between the two dunes. Bayberry, bearberry, cherry, and eastern redcedar grow on the slopes of the dune, while beach grass and heather predominate in the interior of the swale. Descend into the valley and look back toward the forest to notice how the force of the ocean winds has sheared the trees—they slope leeward.

If you wish, walk to the top of the next dune to overlook the ocean, before returning to the trail. The boardwalk leads back into the forest, taking you past stands of winged sumac. This scrubby tree, with its hairy twigs and reddish brown fruit clusters, is characterized by winged midribs on the leaf stems. The fruits are rich in vitamin A, and the whole bush is cropped by deer. In winter, birds occasionally feed on the berries. You'll soon come to the interpretive area, where you turn right and continue back to the visitors' center.

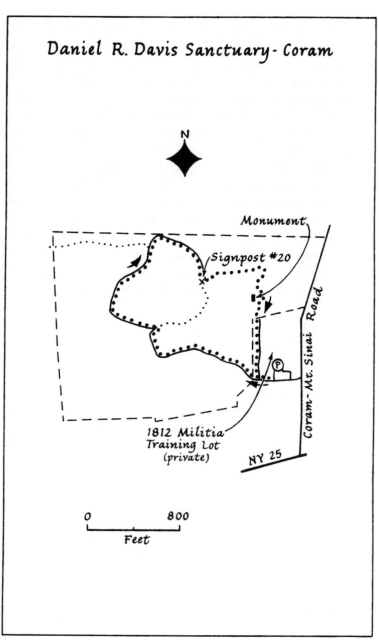

Daniel R. Davis Sanctuary - Coram

N

Monument

Signpost #20

Coram - Mt. Sinai Road

1812 Militia
Training Lot
(private)

NY 25

P

0   800
Feet

Daniel R. Davis Sanctuary

Location: Coram
Owner: The Nature Conservancy
Distance: 1 mile

In spring the lovely song of the hermit thrush can be heard as males stake out nesting territory. In summer the field is ablaze with wildflowers, while autumn brings migrating warblers. Mammals include whitetail deer, red fox, and southern flying squirrel. Nearly 200 species of plants, of which over 150 are flowering, have been recorded within the sanctuary. Be on the lookout for the many different species of oak: chinkapin, dwarf chinkapin, white, chestnut, and scrub. Blueberry, bearberry, and huckleberry also flourish here.

Access

From the Long Island Expressway, take exit 64 north. Continue on NY 112 for 3.4 miles to Coram. Turn right (east) onto NY 25 (Middle Country Road), and proceed 0.2 mile. Turn left (north) onto Mt. Sinai–Coram Road, and go 0.1 mile to a driveway on the left (at #16). The sanctuary driveway is shared with this private drive. There is a small oakleaf preserve sign. Bear right, and go through the gate to the parking area and trailhead. Be sure to close the gate behind you!

Trail

The parking area and part of the preserve abut a field once known as the Training Lot. This field has now "gone to flowers"—it's covered with butterflyweed, milkweed, wood betony, Queen Anne's lace, fleabane, daisy, and a wide variety of grasses. Butterflies frolic and birds feed on this historic War of 1812 drill ground. Although not part of the preserve, the owner has granted an easement, and the trail returns along the field's western edge.

The militia field and preserve entrance

As we stepped out of our car, a pair of northern bobwhite flushed up out of the field. Bobwhites, named for their whistled "bob-bob-WHITE" call, are chunky, reddish brown quail, related to the more often seen ring-necked pheasant. Both species are found in brush, reverting fields, and open woodland. Although once quite common all over Long Island, by 1981 the bobwhite was "bluelisted," meaning that its numbers were dangerously low. Preserves like the Daniel Davis Sanctuary provide a safe haven—food, cover, and nesting sites—for this year-round resident.

Common yellowthroats were singing "witchity-witchity-witch." These tiny (4¼-inch) songbirds are easily distinguished by their unique call. They're also fairly easy to see, since they respond readily to pishing, whistling, and kissing noises. Although the female doesn't have the black face mask of the male, her bright yellow throat is diagnostic. Yellowthroats are probably our most common warbler, and they breed in overgrown fields, woodland margins, hedgerows, and both fresh- and saltwater marshes.

As soon as you enter the wooded area, you'll notice that logs have been placed across the sandy trails; this is to discourage bikers.

Highbush blueberry and locust soon give way to the lowbush blueberry and pitch pine that are indicative of a pine barrens. And this sanctuary's sixty-six acres of pitch pine–scrub oak barrens have high species diversity. It is a haven for some plants that are rapidly disappearing from other areas—such as trailing arbutus and pink lady's slipper. The oak species include scrub oak, chestnut oak, white oak, and chinkapin oak.

You'll first notice the clean, refreshing smell of pine, but as you walk along, you'll see (and smell) evidence of fire. Controlled burning—the Conservancy uses the latest techniques—is used to maintain this plant community, which is naturally dependent on fire.

In some of the burned areas, prairie warblers are singing their ascending "szszsziipp" call. Rufous-sided towhees call "drink-your-tea," or "chewink," their other call. Towhees are large, ground-feeding sparrows, and can be seen scratching in the leaf litter for seeds and fruit. Deeper into the barrens, standing dead oaks provide nesting and feeding sites for hairy woodpeckers. Although similar to its smaller cousin, the downy woodpecker, the hairy has a larger bill; its call is a kingfisher-like rattle or a loud "peek." The hairy woodpecker has an exceptionally long tongue, which wraps around the interior of its skull and is anchored at the base of the bill. The bird inserts its barbed-tipped tongue into tiny holes in tree trunks to extract insects, which form the mainstay (75 to 95 percent) of its diet.

If you are very lucky, you might come upon an eastern hognose snake, a denizen of sandy areas such as this. This snake displays extraordinary behavior. When it feels threatened, it will spread its head, hiss loudly, and inflate its body with air—all to make it appear large and powerful. This show of hostility has earned the hognose snake a bad reputation and some less-than-flattering nicknames (blow viper, for instance). But if you fail to retreat, or if you prod the snake with a stick, it will roll over, open its mouth, convulse, and play dead. The eastern hognose snake is generally about two feet long, and its diet is mostly toads. The hissing, head-spreading, and playing possum are generally sufficient for identification.

At signpost #20, turn left and take the small trail through the woods. You'll go past a monument to the Davises (who donated much of the land for the sanctuary) and come out along the militia training field. Spring azure, common wood nymph, viceroy, and monarch are among the butterflies to be found here.

The viceroy looks like a small version of the monarch, our best-known butterfly. It can be separated from its larger cousin by its smaller size and less powerful wingbeats. Also, the viceroy often glides on flat wings, while the monarch holds its wings in a V. The monarch, half again the size of the viceroy, is a milkweed butterfly, and is famous for its long-distance migration. Monarchs fly along the coast all the way to the mountains of central Mexico, where they overwinter in huge communal roosts. If you pass by the field in late summer, you will likely find these orange-and-black beauties feeding on milkweed.

Wading River Marsh Preserve

Location: Wading River
Owner: The Nature Conservancy
Distance: ¾ mile

There aren't many salt marshes on the North Shore of Long Island—that's a feature found more often on the South Shore, where the sandy terrain slopes gently to broad tidal flats. So Wading River Marsh, flanked on both sides by the 200-foot hills of the Harbor Hill glacial moraine and fed by a freshwater creek, is exceptional in many ways.

Wading River derives its name from the Native American reference *Pauguaconsuk,* which meant "the river where we wade for thick, round-shelled clams." Indeed, when the river was more of a river, Native Americans harvested quahogs and periwinkles from the shellfish flats. But in the natural course of events, the flats were filled in with sand and soil eroding from the surrounding hills, and marsh grasses began to colonize the area.

Today, the marsh is protected from any development (such as drainage) that might have been proposed, but it is still subject to the forces of nature, which for a marsh means it is slowly filling with sediment and the vegetation is getting thicker. We hadn't been to Wading River for some time, and when we revisited it recently, we found it changed: taller trees, bushier undergrowth, and thicker stands of phragmites. It was all the more reason to come here, where the plants and animals of the marsh meet their cousins of the upland.

Access

From exit 68 off the Long Island Expressway take the William Floyd Parkway (County Road 46) north to its end at NY 25A. Turn right (east) and go for 0.75 mile, then turn left onto Randall Road. Take

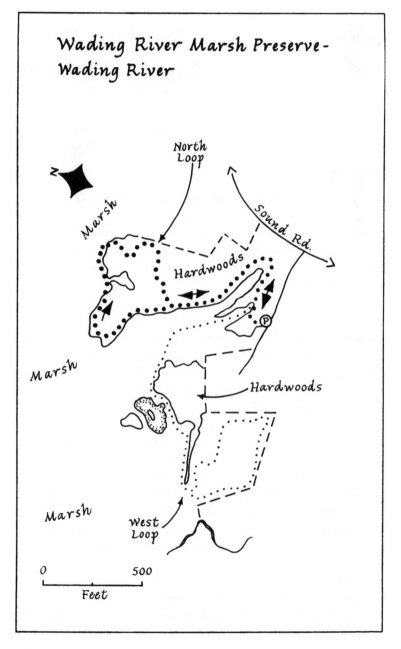

Wading River Marsh Preserve-
Wading River

that to its end at North Country Road, and turn right. Proceed 0.1 mile to the center of Wading River village. At the stop sign, turn left on Sound Avenue and go 0.3 mile to a private drive on the left. The drive is marked by white pillars and a *small* oakleaf sign. Turn in, and proceed about 100 yards to the parking area on the right.

Trail

From the parking lot, follow the entryway to the fork in the trail for the North and West Loops. Both trails skirt the marsh, but we describe the North Loop, as it is better maintained.

The rapid drum of the red-bellied woodpecker is unmistakable here, as is its long rolling "chiv-chiv-chiv" call. Once a bird of more southern climes, the red-bellied has expanded its range northward. The trail is heavy with poison ivy, greenbrier, grape ivy, and wild rose beneath a canopy of mixed oaks and tupelo trees.

The tupelo, or sour gum or black gum, is, like the red-bellied, a species that has migrated north. The alternate simple leaves of the trees are clustered near the ends of the twigs; the flowers—and later the fruits—hang from the stems in bunches of two or three. In fall, the leaves turn a gorgeous deep burgundy. Another way to tell a tupelo is by its dense, nearly horizonal lower branches. It is a tree of swampy woodlands, and it keeps company with red maples, as well as skunk cabbage and ferns. It is along this early part of the trail that you are also likely to see swamp candles—yellow wildflowers with two red spots at the base of each petal; the flowers cluster on an erect stem arising from a whorl of leaves. They bloom from June through August.

The path continues through thickets, with grape ivy covering the holly bushes and Virginia creeper competing with the grape ivy for sunlight. In this woodland setting, listen for gray catbird, tufted titmouse, and especially red-eyed vireo. The vireo is the frustrating "bird in the bush"—it will call almost unceasingly for hours, yet you'll rarely get a glimpse of its trim self among the leaves. The red-eyed's fate is to brood and feed the babies of parasitic brown-headed cowbirds, who lay their eggs in other birds' nests.

Soon the trail traces the edge of the marsh, down past a muddy stretch with phragmites. Phragmites, or common reeds, are a familiar

A view of the marsh

grass of marginal wet areas. Sometimes called plume grass, they bend softly with the breeze, yet to walk among them is to realize how stiff they are. Because they adapt so well, they are often considered invasive, crowding out both woodland and marsh species.

At this point you come close up to the marsh—at water level, almost. A short stretch of ferns bordering the marsh includes the cinnamon, sensitive, royal, lady, and marsh ferns. At marker #7, take the path to the left for an overview—somewhat blocked—of Wading

River Marsh proper. The major grass here is salt marsh cordgrass, *Spartina alterniflora*. In autumn it dies back to the ground, but its underground roots send forth new shoots each spring. Since the grass must have air during part of every tidal cycle and be flooded during other times, the cordgrass grows only between the low-water line and the high-water mark.

Two other grasses, salt meadow grass *(Spartina patens)* and spike grass *(Distichlis spicata)*, grow between the high-water mark and the fringe of the marsh. Essential to a marsh, these grasses filter sediments out of the tidal water and build the soil into a spongy peat. Likewise, when the tides flush the marsh, the decaying plant material washes out to the bay, providing food for marine organisms such as clams and mussels.

Return to the main path and continue on the trail past some unruly grapevines into what seem the dark recesses of the marsh. Do you detect the sweet, musty scent of the marsh? To us it smells "green." Of course, you're still only on the edge. Getting to the heart of a marsh is as difficult to do physically as it is to understand all the life that goes on there. But know that the salt marsh is essential to life on Long Island.

Indeed, a salt marsh is the most productive ecosystem there is. Fully two-thirds of the East Coast's commercial fish catch comes from species that have spent at least part of their lives dependent on the salt marsh. In addition to its importance as a fish nursery, the salt marsh is a source of food for shellfish and a resting and feeding place for birds.

Fiddler crabs and mud snails are abundant invertebrates in the marsh. The fiddler crab, with its one enlarged claw, burrows in the flats and feeds mainly on minute algae and marsh plants. It, in turn, is a mainstay of the clapper rail's diet. The clapper rail, a secretive, chicken-sized bird, breeds in the marsh. Its voice (for which it is named) is a harsh, clacking sound, like a stick being raked across a picket fence. Although it is rarely seen, the high tides occasionally force the bird to come into view.

Along the edge of the marsh, look for tall meadow rue, a summer-flowering wildflower that is favored by bees and butterflies. Lacy and delicate, its leaves resemble a maidenhair fern and its delicate greenish white flowers are in a whorl, with many erect, threadlike stamens dabbed with green. Also likely to be seen is bittersweet nightshade (also known as deadly nightshade), whose violet-and-yellow flower resembles the white-and-yellow flower of the backyard tomato, another nightshade family member. By the way, the plant's toxin isn't fatal but it doesn't exactly taste good, either. Bittersweet nightshade was once used in England to counteract witchcraft.

A candelabrum-shaped tree along the trail is the "lopped tree," the remains of an old-time method of cutting, bending, and tying saplings to act as boundary fences. This one is a hickory estimated to be over 200 years old.

On your return to the parking lot, you are likely to hear the call of the white-eyed vireo, another frustrating "bird in the bush." And if you're quiet and exceptionally lucky, you might see a yellow-billed cuckoo as it glides almost silently from one limb to another. This large bird, known in the South as the rain crow for its habit of calling just before rainstorms, is unrelated to the European cuckoo (of cuckoo clocks). It is a slim, long-tailed bird that is usually well hidden in foliage, favoring dense tangles and moist thickets. The cuckoo's chief food is caterpillars, including the very hairy ones.

Eastern Suffolk

Seashells and boulders

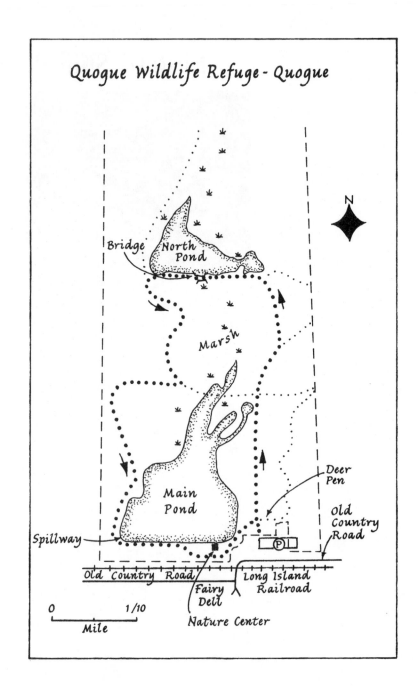

Quogue Wildlife Refuge - Quogue

Bridge

North Pond

Marsh

Main Pond

Spillway

Deer Pen

Old Country Road

Old Country Road

Long Island Railroad

Fairy Dell

Nature Center

N

0   1/10
       Mile

Quogue
Wildlife Refuge

Location: Quogue
Owner: Southampton Township Wildfowl Association
Distance: 1 mile

An irregularity—this swath of green in a sea of farms and fields and houses. A wonderful resource too, where animals are rehabilitated and the land itself is a gift returned to nature. The understory is thick and low, the canopy fairly high, making it easy to spot wildlife and plants: two layers of fringe, full of life. The path is wide and sandy, covered with pine needles, so this is a quiet walk—no crunching leaves to warn of your approach. You meander through blueberry patches, around a pond, over a stream—a private world.

Access

Take NY 27 (Sunrise Highway) to exit 64 south—County Road 104. Continue 2.3 miles to Old Country Road, then turn west (right) and go 0.7 mile to the entrance.

The Charles Banks Belt Nature Center has a library and natural history displays; it's open from February through November on Tuesdays, Thursdays, Saturdays, and Sundays 1 PM to 4 PM. A huge picture window overlooks Main Pond; binoculars and spotting scopes are available for visitors to use. The refuge is open every day, year-round, from 9 AM to 5 PM. Picnicking is not allowed in the refuge. Restrooms, located near the deer pen at the beginning of the main trail, are open from spring through fall.

Across the railroad tracks from the refuge entrance is the historic Fairy Dell estuarine tract. This area is traversed by a ¼-mile boardwalk trail that accommodates wheelchairs. Wheelchair users might also enjoy bird-watching from the nature center. The nature

Box turtle

trail at the refuge is mostly sand and woodchips, and would be rough going for wheelchairs. We've chosen to describe the nature trail; there are other trails as well.

Trail

This 200-acre reserve encompasses the headwaters of Quantuck Creek. The land was originally owned by the Quogue Ice Company, which built the eleven-acre Main Pond specifically for ice harvesting. The availability of mechanical refrigeration by the mid-1920s, however, spelled the end for the ice-cutting industry. (A display of the ice-harvesting industry is located in an old barn near the nature study center.)

The ponds are now home to a variety of waterfowl, and as you enter the preserve you'll walk among a flock of Canada geese and mallards looking for handouts. Perhaps you'll notice the many shades of green in both the canopy and the understory: pitch pine, white oak, scrub oak, highbush blueberry, and jack-in-the-pulpit.

American holly—yet a different shade of green—grows near the deer pen. Whitetail deer are the only native ungulates (grazing animals, like cows) on Long Island. There is usually one or more deer being rehabilitated here. Frequently fawns are brought to the center by well-meaning people who think they've rescued an orphan because they found it by itself. It is best to leave all wild young alone unless you're absolutely sure that they are in distress. If you're quiet, and fortunate, you'll see deer along the trail, as we did.

As you leave the pine-oak woodlands (and come to a T in the trail), the landscape opens out. The large birdhouses in the field to the right are for purple martins—our largest swallow. These gregarious birds are colonial nesters and prefer a multifamily dwelling. The male martin is a steely violet blue-black, while the female has a bluish brown back and white underparts. Purple martins are exclusively insect-eating, and it has been said that one bird will consume 2,000 mosquitoes in a day, all of them caught on the wing. (They also eat flies, beetles, moths, ants, wasps, dragonflies, and spiders.) The birds arrive in April, flying north from their wintering grounds in South America. Martins like to nest in open country, especially near water, so Quogue Refuge is ideal.

If you turn left at the crossroad, you'll soon come upon a marshy area and the north end of the Main Pond. "Witchity-witchity-witch!" is the sharp call of the common yellowthroat, a small warbler with an olive back, black mask, and yellow throat. This is a bird typical of marshy areas, and it can easily be whistled (or pished) into the open. While on the little bridge here, you might see a northern oriole fly over. They, too, like to be near water. And don't forget to look down as well. You'll see some of the native warm-water fish community—bass, sunfish, catfish, pickerel, and perhaps an eel. Painted and snapping turtles, too, live in this ecotone, as do myriad insects. Whirligig beetles, water boatmen, water striders, and backswimmers, as their names suggest, spend their entire lives in the water.

The highly acidic state of the freshwater bog causes decomposition to occur very slowly, depriving the plants of nutrients that they need. So the bog plant community has found ways to adapt. Some plants—like the pitcher plant, sundew, and bladderwort—are insectivorous. Sphagnum moss, a dominant and essential bog plant, has the ability to hold about 400 times its own weight in water! This water-holding quality of the moss allows other bog plants—like cottongrass, swamp azalea, and some orchids—to thrive.

A lovely purplish red flower stands tall on a stalk amid a grouping of pitchers. When disturbed, the flower gives off an unpleasant odor. The pitchers—actually the leaves of the plant—are filled with liquid. We sit there, waiting for an insect to drop in. Dragonflies dart across the bog like miniature jewels, heedless of danger.

On the other side of the bridge, water lilies float in the pond. As you continue along the trail you enter a pine forest. Rufous-sided towhees scratch among the pine needles on the forest floor. Note their characteristic double-scratch foraging technique. A towhee's nest is often just a cup-shaped depression, the rim flush with the ground surface. The nest is lined with fine grass and hair. Three or four grayish (or creamy white) eggs are laid; the nestlings are brooded by the female, and the male feeds them. To distract predators from the nest the female towhee occasionally feigns injury. Other animals that live on or near the forest floor are chipmunks, voles, shrews, and fox.

As you round the bend by the south end of the Main Pond, remember that, because the pond was created for ice harvesting, it's only three to five feet deep. The gravel spots you see in the pond in late spring and early summer are sunfish nests. Year-round waterfowl seen regularly here include wood duck, American black duck, and mallard; in winter you can also see hooded merganser, northern pintail, and northern shoveler. Migratory ducks include ring-necked, canvasback, green-winged teal, and gadwall.

The spillway here was constructed to control the water level in the pond. If you walk onto the platform behind you, you can see snapping turtle, fish, and, sometimes, sponge. A gray, jellylike mass, sponge is an extremely primitive life form, yet one that's been around for about 500 million years.

The trail continues through a swampy area—look for skunk cabbage in early spring—back to the nature center.

David A. Sarnoff
Pine Barrens Preserve

Location: Riverhead
Owner: New York State
Distance: ¾ mile

As we write, a forest fire has burned 3,500 acres of the pine barrens near Rocky Point; another is raging out of control just north of Westhampton. The entire pine barrens of Suffolk County is a tinderbox, awaiting the spark to create a broom of flames that will sweep first in one direction, then in another, pushed by stiff winds. This has been a dry summer, and it's several years since a forest fire has burned away the leaf litter and scorched the trees of their top growth. It's time for renewal. Fire is a natural part of pine barrens ecology. We can enjoy a walk through an area like the David Sarnoff Preserve, but unless we acknowledge the role of fire here, we can never really understand the pine barrens of Long Island. The Sarnoff Preserve, part of the new Pine Barrens State Forest Preserve, is a 2,056-acre area just outside of Riverhead.

Access

From exit 71 of the Long Island Expressway, take NY 24 (also called County Road 94) south to the Riverhead traffic circle. Then make your first right onto County Road 63 (Lake Avenue), and go south for 0.2 mile. The preserve entrance is signposted on the left. There is a small parking lot; otherwise there are no public facilities.

There is a Pine Barrens Visitors' Center in Manorville, just north of exit 70 (off the L.I.E.), on the right. It's open Friday through Monday from 9:30 AM to 5:30 PM. There are exhibits, displays, and information about the pine barrens.

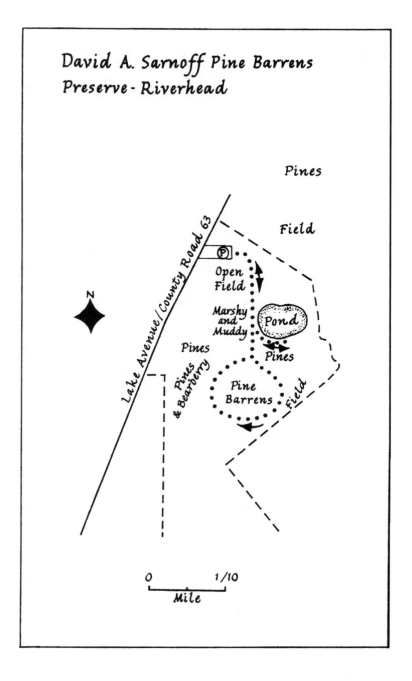

David A. Sarnoff Pine Barrens
Preserve - Riverhead

Trail

There are three trails, but the one to Frog Pond is a casual stroll through lovely pine barrens woodland. This forest of mixed oaks and pitch pine grows from a sandy, acidic soil that also supports a ground cover of bearberry and some prickly pear, especially at the beginning of the trail. Prickly pear is the only cactus native to Long Island. Its flat, fleshy pads are covered with clusters of short, barbed bristles. When it flowers, any time from May to August, the showy yellow blooms are sure to get your attention. Later, the plant produces large greenish purple fruits that are edible.

Early residents of the pine barrens harvested the prickly pears, as well as the cranberries, huckleberries, and blueberries that grow here and that you'll see along the trail. For even though this part of Long Island was viewed as virtually a wasteland—hence the name *pine barrens*—the unique habitat is far from "barren." Additionally, the central pine barrens is an immense recharge area—essentially a large sponge—for Long Island's water supply.

Also along the trail is bayberry, an evergreen shrub with alternate, short-stemmed leaves. It is most easy to recognize by the clusters of tiny, waxy, blue-gray berries on the stems. Both the leaves and the berries are aromatic when crushed; the berries are used for candle making, but bear in mind that it takes 1½ quarts to make an eight-inch candle!

In the shade of the trees, you're likely to see brown thrashers and robins, as well as gray catbirds, towhees, and perhaps some thrushes. Look down as well, and you'll see spotted wintergreen growing. A perennial plant, spotted wintergreen sends a flower stalk up from its base of green leaves mottled with white. The flowers are fragrant, usually two white nodding bells perched about three inches above the leaves. It flowers from June to August, and seems to set seed best after a wildfire.

Bracken fern is another pine barrens standby, and it is here at David Sarnoff as well. It is a strong and coarse fern, one of the earliest to appear in spring, and it continues through the season. Shunning areas with moist, rich soil—places that most other ferns relish—the bracken prefers burned-over spots and sandy, semishaded locations.

The master of the pine barrens is the pitch pine tree, which is well represented here. A stocky tree with thick, insulating bark, the pitch pine grows awkwardly, often acquiring lopsided or twisted shapes that seem ghoulish. The tight cones of the tree are quite small, and they often hang on the branches for several years like worn-out Christmas ornaments. At one time these pines grew tall and full; ship captains long ago mentioned smelling the fragrance of the trees from more than a hundred miles at sea. But harvesting for charcoal and turpentine, plus competition from intruding scrub oaks and other vegetation, has reduced the pitch pines to short, stubby trees. Yet the value of the pitch pine is in its ability, after a forest fire, to sprout new shoots from its charred base and lower trunk—an adaptation many other trees do not have.

The pitch pine, as well as scrub oaks, huckleberries, blueberries, and some other pine barrens plants, is able to recover from even a devastating forest fire. Indeed, pine barrens are not only fire-adapted, they are also fire-dependent. As the pines age, their ability to produce seeds decreases. The forest fire is a shot at rejuvenation, a chance to grow new sprouts that will produce healthy cones full of seeds. When the leaf litter is burned off, those seeds can germinate in the exposed soil, drawing nutrients and minerals, some of which have been deposited by the ash. So as you walk down the path that leads to and goes alongside the pond, consider that what you see is both temporary and eternal: temporary because a forest fire may well sweep through here tomorrow, eternal in its pattern of fire and rebirth.

Another ecological tale begins at the pond, a boggy depression in the otherwise sandy soil of the pine barrens. Off the trail is a path that leads down to the pond, where the white fragrant water lilies bloom, usually from early morning until noon, from June through September. Green frogs are abundant here; their voice has been described as a loose banjo string, rather explosive as either a single note or repeated three or four times. Green frogs breed from April through August. Because they are fine leapers, you may see them jumping off a lily pad into the water.

Along the edge of the pond look for round-leafed sundews, insectivorous plants whose round, reddish leaves sprout sticky glan-

Pine barrens habitat

dular hairs that ensnare insects. The mud borders of the pond show the tracks of deer, fox, and raccoons. A killdeer—a large (10½-inch) plover recognized by its double black breast bands—announces its presence with a piercing "kill-dee." Though commonly seen in meadows and short-grass fields, the killdeer also feeds along river and pond banks. Likewise, the pond attracts green herons, which skulk among the grasses or sit quietly on a twig overhanging the water.

After viewing the pond, return to the path. At a T-intersection you can go either way, as the path here makes a circle. A burned-out building, off to one side of the trail, is an unattractive remnant of human habitation.

You'll return to this same intersection and retrace your steps past the pond and back to the trailhead.

Cranberry Bog County Nature Preserve

Location: Riverhead
Owner: Suffolk County
Distance: 1¼ miles

Local history is rarely isolated from natural history. So it is that the Cranberry Bog County Nature Preserve has evidence of Long Island's once thriving cranberry industry as well as a still vigorous 390-acre freshwater wetland natural community.

Here, where people a century ago flooded the bog and harvested tons of cranberries, can be found some of Long Island's more unusual plants, such as carnivorous sundews and delicate orchids, as well as migrating waterfowl, mink, frogs, and snakes. Tucked away in the pine barrens of Suffolk County, the bog is a place of solitude.

Access

Take exit 71 off the Long Island Expressway. Follow NY 24 (also called County Road 94) south to the Riverhead traffic circle. Take County Road 63 (Lake Avenue, the first right off the circle) south for 0.9 mile. The preserve entrance is at an unmarked, locked gate on the right.

Park off the road, but do not block the gate. There is foot access only.

Trail

Walk in along what was an old entry road. This wide path is lined with bearberry, a member of the heath family. The low, trailing evergreen is an attractive ground cover, and you'll be seeing it increasingly for sale at garden centers. With rounded, smooth, leathery green leaves and red stems, the bearberry has a white bell-shaped flower in

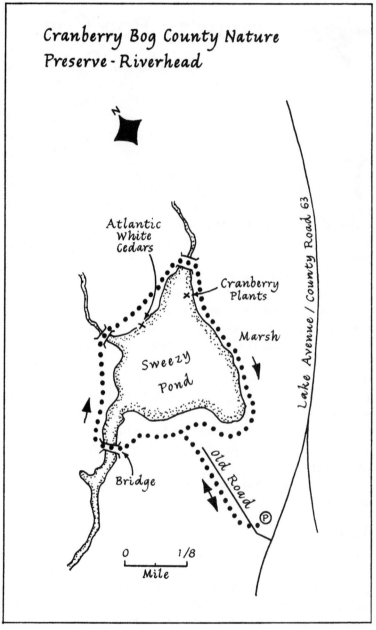

Cranberry Bog County Nature Preserve - Riverhead

N

Atlantic White Cedars

Cranberry Plants

Marsh

Sweezy Pond

Bridge

Old Road

Lake Avenue / County Road 63

P

0   1/8
Mile

Bearberry

May or June and round red berries in the fall. We've heard that a tart tea is made from the dried leaves. The berry is edible, too; although tasteless to us, it is loved by birds.

This is pine barrens, so many of the trees here are pitch pine and oaks. The soil is sandy. As you near the pond, you'll find the plants that require more moisture, such as red maple and sweet pepperbush, whose dried seed pods resemble black peppercorns. Sweezy Pond opens before you—a boggy, shallow depression with intermittent tussocks of grasses and ferns. In the shallows at the water's edge is pickerelweed, with its lovely spikes of violet flowers and funnel-like, long green leaves. The seeds of the pickerelweed apparently can be eaten like nuts and the young leaf stalks can be cooked as greens (although collecting plants from this—or any—nature preserve is strictly forbidden).

Sweezy Pond is part of the former Woodhull bog, one of the biggest cranberry operations on Long Island. From the late 1880s to the 1930s, the sand and bog margins of the Peconic River produced thousands of bushels of cranberries each year—indeed, at that time Suffolk County was the third largest producer of cranberries in the nation, behind Massachusetts and New Jersey. A variety of problems brought an end to the local industry but left a habitat that's being reclaimed by the plants and animals that are most at home in a water-saturated environment.

Take the trail to the left around the pond, until you reach a little bridge over a narrow lagoon. Look among the wild roses, swamp azalea, cinnamon ferns, and bog willow for the diminutive yellow warbler, whose abundant presence is confirmed by its "sweet, sweet, I'm so sweet" song. Here, too, picking its way among the lily pads, may well be the green heron, a solitary hunter that slowly stalks its prey or crouches and waits for food to swim by.

The cinnamon fern is one of our most common and prominent ferns, especially in moist soils. It's first to appear in the spring and first to turn its bright green leaves to cinnamon brown in summer. The spore cases also turn cinnamon, and the stalks are covered with a cinnamon tan wool. People once thought that carrying fern seed gave the gift of invisibility, perhaps because the spores are so tiny.

Dragonflies and damselflies will likely be out hunting, seizing tiny insect prey in midair. Though superficially similar, they are not difficult to tell apart. Dragonflies are larger, with fatter bodies, and they hold their wings out to the sides. The smaller damselflies are able to hold their wings up vertically when at rest. Both have four powerful wings that move independently, enabling them to fly both forward and backward, as well as hover.

Compared to most insects, dragonflies and damselflies are considered primitive—older in terms of evolution—because they cannot protect their wings by folding them against their bodies, as can, say, a housefly. On the other hand, they have 30,000 lenses in their eyes, so they can really see details! There are 450 species of dragonflies and damselflies in North America, including garners, gomphids, and skimmers.

Stoop down and look closely at the boggy earth at the pond edge. Insectivorous plants like sundews and pitcher plants will be making themselves appealing to curious insects. These plants generally grow in poor soil, so they must derive extra nutrition from the insects they catch. The round-leafed sundew, with its basal arrangement of small, round, reddish leaves, is found here. Often these plants will send up a single leafless stalk, topped with a cluster of white flowers. But it's the sticky, hairy leaves that are the trap; woe to the tiny bug that lands on those sticky hairs!

The trail follows around the pond, moving onto slightly higher ground where trees such as tupelo, red maple, and eastern redcedar grow. Along the trail you'll also pass some paper birch trees and some Atlantic white cedars. The papery white bark of the paper birch is a giveaway in its identification, and always a dramatic sight along a trail. It's a tree that grows quickly when an area has been burned or cleared, an opportunistic species, as is the eastern redcedar.

A juniper—not a true cedar—the eastern redcedar produces bluish white seeds that birds, especially cedar waxwings, love to eat. Mostly, the tree is a spire, resembling the cypress trees of the Mediterranean. Its branches form a tight mass that makes a safe haven for roosting small owls and other birds. One of its distinctive characteristics is that two forms of the leaves can occur, even on the same branch: awl-shaped and scale-shaped. For many years the redcedar was harvested for pencil wood, but that eventually proved unprofitable.

The Atlantic white cedars here are true cedars—some of the last of their kind on Long Island. This conical evergreen with an open, flat, fan-shaped spray is often confused with the arborvitae, an introduced cultivated plant grown in suburban yards for privacy. But while the cones of the white cedar are tiny round balls with knobs, the arborvitae's are oblong with scales. We find white cedar easiest to identify by noting how the bark twists around the trunk, the way socks get twisted around the ankles when the elastic's gone.

The cedar was a favorite of loggers, harvested heavily for fence posts, piles, log cabins, telegraph poles, and shingles. It has been said that the rain falling on a roof of cedar shingles sounded in varying pitches, inspiring an organ builder to use the wood for pipe organs. There aren't many Atlantic white cedars left in our area—mostly a southern species, there never were large stands. But in addition to lumber harvesting, the cedars were often killed when bogs were flooded for cranberry cultivation.

The understory in the area behind the pond is a collection of blueberry, bayberry, sheep laurel, cherry, and young sassafras. Check the ground, however, to see the spreading vines of cranberries. In June and early July, look among the short, shiny leaves (green above, white below) for the tiny white flowers whose four petals fold backward from a red center, like a shooting star. In late September and early October, you'll see the bright red berries instead.

For commercial cultivation, the cranberry vines must grow in a bed of sand in the bog. Dikes of sand were built up around the cranberry bog, so that the bog could be flooded after harvest to protect the plants from freezing in winter. In spring, the bogs were drained, then covered with about four inches of fresh sand, which encouraged new growth. After harvest, the bogs were flooded again for winter. To the left of the trail you'll see the pits from which the sand was dug for the Woodhull bog. Also along the trail you'll pass the remains of a pump house from the cranberry operation.

As you pass around the back end of Sweezy Pond, keep on the lookout for other wet-area wildflowers, such as starflower and swamp dewberry. Starflower is aptly named: seven pure white petals are perched in a circle on a fragile stem that rises from a whorl of small green leaves. It flowers from late spring through late summer, and brightens the margins of the leaf-strewn path. Swamp dewberry's simple five-petaled white flower gives itself away as a member of the rose family. Look for the backward-pointed bristles and erect branches with shiny leaves in groups of three. The fruit can be red or blackish and looks like a blackberry. This is a creeper, getting no higher than twelve inches, but it is a very important summer plant food for songbirds. The trail ends where you began, at the junction with the wide road to the entry gate.

Penny Pond

Location: Flanders
Owner: Suffolk County
Distance: 1 mile

J ust east of Riverhead, along the northern shore of the South
Fork, the coastline juts up slightly to separate Flanders Bay
from Great Peconic Bay. Stretching from the shore inland
almost to Sunrise Highway is a vast area of mostly undeveloped
land—a rare commodity on Long Island. How lovely it is that Hubbard
County Park, and the adjacent Sears Bellows County Park, helps
preserve such a large part of our critical pine barrens.

Hubbard County Park is spread out over 1,200 acres and has
few signs and no formal facilities. But because the park is laced with
trails, you can explore much of this little-known area without meeting
other people or hearing cars, leafblowers, and other scourges of modern life. The walk to Penny Pond is particularly refreshing, passing
through a typical pitch pine and mixed oak woods to reach a secluded
lily pond with crystal-clear water.

Access

From Sunrise Highway (NY 27), take exit 65 north, toward Riverhead.
Go north on NY 24 for 2 miles and turn right on Red Creek Road.
Go 1.1 miles, bearing right at the fork, to a small pull-off on the right.
There are two low concrete pillars with a bar across them. Park here,
but don't block the roadway.

Trail

As you walk down the sandy dirt road toward the pond, you're likely
to hear the "drink-your-tea" song of the rufous-sided towhee. Named
for its call note, "tow-whee," which is heard less often, the towhee
favors brushy areas and open woodlands with a leafy ground cover.
You may even see the towhee as it scratches among the leaves,

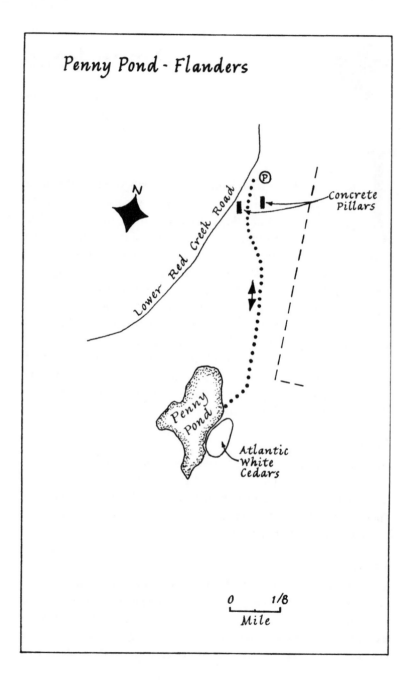

Penny Pond - Flanders

Lower Red Creek Road

Concrete Pillars

Penny Pond

Atlantic White Cedars

N

0   1/8
Mile

unearthing bugs and seeds for its nestlings or itself. The male is black above, with a black hood, chestnut sides, and white underparts; the female is brown above and has a brown hood. Both sexes have a bright red eye.

This part of the pine barrens represents a transitional zone between the rocky Harbor Hill terminal moraine that forms the spine of the North Fork and the Ronkonkoma moraine that extends out to Montauk. There is a bit more loam to the soil here, although it is still largely sand, of a poor quality, and has a high acid content. The primary trees that can be seen along the trail are pitch pine and oaks, while the understory is blueberry bushes.

Pitch pines are easily recognized by their short, thick trunks and whorled, contorted branches. But check the needle cluster; there should be three to a bundle, about three inches long. In early times, tar, pitch, and turpentine were extracted from the knots of pitch pines, hence their name; indeed, the tar derived from pitch pine was considered the best axle grease for wagons. Full of resin, the knots of pitch pine were lit as torches in the woods. And the coarse-grained wood was used for building barns, wharves, waterwheels, and other structures where the wood's great resistance to water damage was important.

The pitch pine is a testament to survival. It grows in the poorest of soils, even along salt-soaked seashores. Its dark, tightly closed cones hold fast to the limbs for years, even aging to a dull gray. But most notably, the pitch pine will easily survive a forest fire, the only pine to sprout fresh green growth from its stems and stump.

The oaks along the path are a mixture of white, scarlet, and chestnut oaks. The white oaks can most easily be recognized by their vertical blocks of scaly gray bark and long leaves with rounded lobes. In summer, the yellow flowers on the stem just below some emerging red leaves are especially obvious. These trees are stately, and in better soil conditions would reach magnificent heights. The scarlet oak's leaves are deeply cut to the midrib, almost skeletal; they turn a brilliant scarlet in fall. Chestnut oak leaves, in contrast, are large with wavy edges; the undersides often are hairy. The chestnut oak's acorns germinate quickly, scarcely hitting the ground before they sprout.

You may smell a musky odor—what at first seems to be a skunk, but not nearly as penetrating. Skunks are very rare on Long Island; what you detect is a fox. These woods are a prime area for red fox. At one time, they were common all over Long Island, well into eastern Queens. Red fox are still found throughout eastern Nassau and Suffolk Counties, but seeing them is not always easy. Clever, perky, and adaptive, the red fox runs with its head high and its ears pricked up. The fur is reddish yellow, the tail tipped with white, and the legs and feet black. On your walk to the pond you might spot one. Likely, it will have been searching for mice or berries.

At the end of the trail is Penny Pond, a large kettle hole. On Long Island, huge blocks of glacial ice remained on the land surface between the two moraines, and were buried in outwash (soil and gravel) coming from the Harbor Hill moraine. As the ice blocks melted, the outwash collapsed, leaving depressions in the land called kettle holes.

The pond today is fed by groundwater seepage and rainfall, and is home to largemouth bass, bluegill, and pickerel. In fact, the road you have walked down is used by anglers as well, who have permission to launch their boats here. However, fishing activity is modest and low-key, and not likely to mar the peaceful scene.

At the shore's edge are water plants such as pickerelweed, with its violet-blue flower spikes and heart-shaped, tapering leaves. A little farther out are fragrant water lilies and yellow pond lilies. The pond lily's globe-shaped bloom stands above its leaves, while the water lily's white flowers are at surface level. The leaves and blooms of both plants die back each year and contribute to the organic matter in the pond.

The red maples ringing the pond are easy to spot: look for red stems and red buds. As Thoreau noted, the red maple's "virtues, not its sins, are as scarlet." Note the stands of Atlantic white cedar at scattered sites around the pond. Perfuming the air in summer is the white-flowered swamp azalea, sometimes called swamp honeysuckle. Lichens such as British soldiers, reindeer moss, and pixie cup also grow here. Overhead, red-winged blackbirds flash their scarlet shoulder patches, calling "koo-ka-reee" to announce their territories. Goldfinches, which in breeding season are a neon yellow with black cap

View of the pond with water lilies

and wings, sing a lively series of trills and twitters—a good reason why they are sometimes called "wild canaries." Although the path is a bit overgrown, it may be possible to go at least partly around the pond, if you wish the additional walk. (For best results, begin to the right of where the trail meets the pond.) In any event, you follow the same trail back to the entry gate.

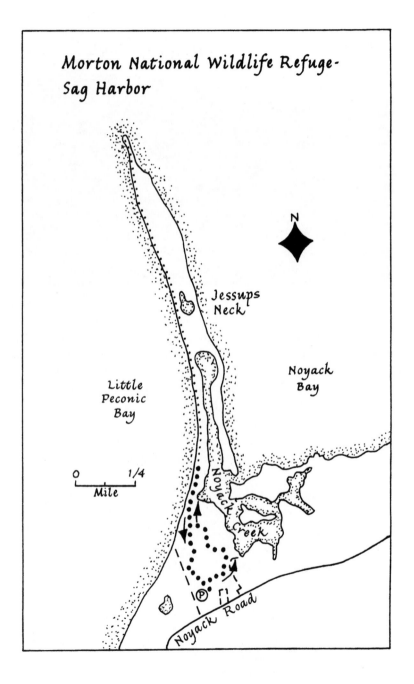

Morton National Wildlife Refuge-
Sag Harbor

N

Jessups
Neck

Noyack
Bay

Little
Peconic
Bay

0   1/4
Mile

Noyack Creek

P

Noyack Road

Morton National Wildlife Refuge

Location: Sag Harbor
Owner: U.S. Fish and Wildlife Service
Distance: 1½ miles

Light as a feather, a butterfly kiss of tiny feet. A black-capped chickadee lands on your fingertips. In a flash, it picks a sunflower seed from your palm and is gone. There it is: in a honeysuckle vine, eating. Another eyes you from a nearby limb, makes a pass at your hand, but flies off. Bright-eyes is back, copping another seed. Gone. "Dee-dee-dee." You stand there, arm extended, immobile. Seed clings to the sweat on your palm. You hope for another chickadee to come. One is just above your hand, checking you out, but a different one swoops in from the left and alights just long enough to pick out a snack. It's the thrill of a lifetime.

Access

From the town of Sag Harbor, take Main Street south to Brick Kiln Road; turn right (west) on Brick Kiln Road and go 2 blocks to Noyack Road. Turn right (west) on Noyack Road and proceed to the entrance (about 4.5 miles). The preserve is open daylight hours, year-round.

Facilities include public toilets and a small picnic area, located at an information kiosk. It's become a local tradition to feed the chickadees at Morton. Hand-feeding of the birds is usually done just behind the buildings, but there is no seed for sale—you have to bring your own. *Be sure to use only unsalted sunflower seeds; salt is harmful to the birds.* Although unpaved, the terrain in this area is relatively flat and wheelchair accessible.

Trail

Begin at the information kiosk and take the first path to the right. This is the beginning of a ¾-mile loop trail. You're sure to notice the

Hand-feeding the chickadees

big eastern redcedar on the right side of the trail. Redcedar is a pioneer tree, often found growing where there were once old fields. The thickets here are largely composed of greenbrier, bittersweet, and honeysuckle, all massing in a huge tangle.

This area, just behind the buildings, is the best place to hand-feed the birds. In addition to the chickadees, tufted titmice will come to your hand, as will the occasional white-breasted nuthatch. Northern cardinals walk out in the path, picking up dropped seeds, while winter wrens scold from deep inside the briary thickets. When feeding the birds it's important to remain as motionless as possible and to have the seeds visible in the palm of your hand. It may take some time for a bird to gain the confidence to come to you, so be patient—although, as one six-year-old told us, "You can eat the seed too."

Chickadees are extraordinary creatures: they can grow new brain cells, and they do so in fall to locate food. They are resident birds; and who is not cheered in winter by their friendly "chick-a-dee-dee-dee" call? Although they don't nest colonially, they do form small flocks in winter; up to a dozen individuals will forage and roost together.

After the feeding extravaganza, continue along the loop trail, which leads through woodland, brush, and open fields. You'll pass a small stream and marsh. Here you're liable to run into a small flock of guineafowl. They look like big, gray chickens, and are easily told by their high squeaks. These are escaped birds that have become feral. A pond on the left has a birdhouse (for tree swallows) and is ringed by phragmites. The tree swallows left for Central America in September, but will be back again by April.

The path climbs slightly and opens onto a field. Here are bluebird houses and an osprey platform. The eastern bluebird is New York's state bird and is making quite a comeback on Long Island.

At a T-intersection, turn right. This will take you to the beach, and is ¼ mile each way. Northern red, white, and post oaks dominate the woodland, but soon the vegetation thins out and trees appear stunted. This is due to the forces of strong, salty winds. The trail opens to the beach and gives views of Jessups Neck, the peninsula beyond. The sandy and pebbly beach provides views of Little Peconic Bay to the west and Noyack Bay to the east. Osprey regularly nest on platforms set along the shore.

Jessups Neck occupies two-thirds of the 187-acre refuge, and its sandy, rocky, and gravelly beaches are a nesting area for endangered birds such as least tern and piping plover. As such, public access to the peninsula is prohibited during breeding season (April through August). As recently as the early 1950s, the least tern was known as the most abundant tern of the region. For a while it faced an uncertain future because its nest sites—sandy beaches—were also the places favored by real estate developers and beachgoers. Now that the bird has received federal protection, it might stand a chance.

We have three species of tern breeding on Long Island: common, roseate, and least. The least, as you may expect, is the smallest. About the size of a catbird, the least tern has a black cap and a yellow bill. Commons have red bills, and roseates' bills are black.

The sand here is white and as fine as sugar, with tiny pebbles and shells—mostly scallops, periwinkles, slippers, mussels, and jingle shells. Jingle shells are bivalves; their shells are translucent and glossy, about an inch or two wide. The shell color is highly variable, ranging from white to brown. The ones found here are mostly yellow and orange.

Down the spine of the peninsula are bluffs, some up to fifty feet high. But prevailing winds from the southwest have gullied them considerably. There is less damage on the eastern side, where the bluffs support some vegetation—bayberry, honeysuckle, and some shrubs.

In the winter the bays fill up with ducks: goldeneye, bufflehead, scoters (all three species), canvasback, greater and lesser scaups, American black duck, mallard, northern pintail, long-tailed duck (oldsquaw), and red-breasted merganser. November and December are the best months for spotting common loon and horned grebe. Loons are resident and in April can be heard calling. Stand on the beach near sunset and listen for them.

In fall and winter, you can hike to the tip of the peninsula, 2 miles each way. Out at the point, but also in Little Peconic Bay, you can see wintering harbor seals.

Retrace your steps to the intersection and continue straight ahead. Bitternut and pignut hickory dominate, along with the oaks. An easy way to separate the hickories is by their nuts: the bitternut has ribbed nuts, while those of the pignut are smooth. Both, of course, are food for the birds and mammals of the refuge. Over 220 species of birds have been recorded here; mammals include red fox, longtail weasel, eastern cottontail rabbit, opossum, raccoon, and whitetail deer. Although chiefly nocturnal, weasels can be seen in the daytime, usually around the improved areas.

Mashomack
Preserve

Location: Shelter Island
Owner: The Nature Conservancy
Distance: 1½ miles

Mashomack is a showcase, a dream, a miniwilderness in the midst of civilization. Its 2,000 acres seem an extravagance in such a popular and populated part of the world. Two thousand acres! The potential is here for daylong walks through woods and meadow, shore and marsh. At Mashomack you can walk unimpeded and undisturbed by the trappings of twentieth-century life. Though there are some signs of human effort, much of the landscape is natural or reverting. A walk in Mashomack is a walk up and down the remnants of glaciers that passed through thousands of years ago.

Access

From Sag Harbor, take the South Ferry to Shelter Island. Upon landing, drive north on NY 114 for 1 mile to the preserve entrance.

From Greenport, take the North Ferry, then follow NY 114 south for 3 miles to the entrance. The preserve is open daily, except Tuesdays, from 9 AM to 5 PM. A visitors' center houses natural history displays, a gift shop, and public restrooms. Adjacent to the visitors' center building are a small picnic area and a native plant garden.

Although the main trails might be tough going in a wheelchair, there is a service road that could be used. In addition, there is a 1,500-foot boardwalk trail for the handicapped, with interpretive signs that are also in Braille.

The suggested donation for visiting Mashomack is $1.50 per person.

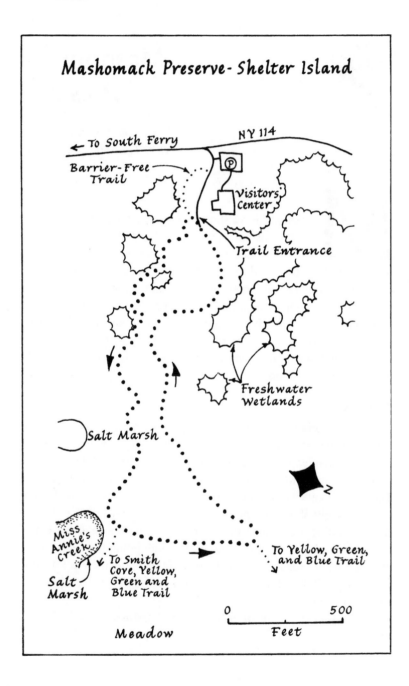

Mashomack Preserve-Shelter Island

NY 114

← To South Ferry

Barrier-Free Trail

Visitors Center

Trail Entrance

Freshwater Wetlands

Salt Marsh

Miss Annie's Creek

Salt Marsh

To Smith Cove, Yellow, Green and Blue Trail

To Yellow, Green, and Blue Trail

Meadow

0   500
        Feet

Trail

There are several trails at Mashomack, but we've chosen to describe the Red Trail, which is a 1½-mile loop to and from the visitors' center. The others (Yellow, Green, and Blue) are connected, either to the Red Trail or to each other, in ever-widening loops. Taken together, the Red and Yellow Trails are 3 miles, and traverse a variety of habitats, while the Blue Trail is 11 miles and goes all the way to Gardiners Bay.

Your first view of Mashomack—jewel of the Peconic—is likely to be the osprey nest near the South Ferry landing. If there is any one creature that typifies the wild spirit of Mashomack, it is the osprey. This is one of the largest nesting osprey colonies in the Northeast, numbering a dozen pairs.

After you leave the visitors' center, you'll enter a dappled oak-beech forest. Soon you're atop a small hill, which affords a view of the treetops. This hill is called a kame, and it was formed about 15,000 years ago, during the Wisconsin Ice Age. Small ponds occupy the lower areas; otherwise the forest is dry. These depressions (called kettle holes) were made by huge blocks of glacial ice. Spotted salamanders use these pools for breeding sites. Deep in the woodlands, you may spot the pink lady's slipper or whorled pogonia—two state-protected orchids that can be found along the path. (A small cage at signpost #2 protects a lady's slipper from danger.)

A little farther along you enter a wet forest whose inhabitants' roots are embedded in bog and water. This is the realm of the red maple. You can easily tell a red maple because some part of the tree is always red: in winter the buds are scarlet; in spring, red flowers appear; in summer the leafstalks are red; and in fall the leaves become crimson. Tupelo, also known as black gum, is another tree characteristic of freshwater swamps. The understory here is composed of sweet-smelling swamp azalea and sweet pepperbush. Bog willow surrounds most of the swamp; its purple flowers bloom late in summer. The floating vegetation that you see are various species of duckweed. Look here for eastern kingbirds as they sally out, catching insects. This large tyrant flycatcher is easy to spot: it's dark above and white below, and it will perch out on an open twig. Another fly-

Whitetail deer

catcher seen here is the eastern phoebe. Unlike the kingbird, the phoebe wags its tail after it lands on an exposed perch. Barn and tree swallows sail gracefully over the marsh, catching insects on the wing. Spotted and eastern painted turtles can be seen sunning themselves on dead logs. The big ferns are cinnamon ferns, so named for their cinnamon-colored stalks.

When the trail turns left, it climbs back up, and soon you're in a grove of black locust trees. The locust is easily identified by its deeply grooved bark and its compound leaves with oval leaflets. Its white flowers, which bloom in the summer, are very sweet smelling. Locusts are durable (they resist both insects and rot), and these groves were planted here by Colonial farmers for use in building. But they are also shade intolerant, so, as the forest ages, they will die out.

As the trail winds closer to the water, the woodland yields to coastal marsh. A gazebo overlooks a yellow-green field of salt meadow grass waving in the breeze. This is an appropriate place to stop and take a rest. The open water ahead is Smith Cove, across from which is the South Ferry. This is but a part of Mashomack's ten miles of coastline. Great and snowy egrets, great blue heron, green heron, and greater yellowlegs are among the waders and shorebirds to be seen here, poking around for food. In late fall migrating ducks arrive, and in the winter months you can see American black ducks, buffleheads, and red-breasted mergansers. Mergansers, commonly called sawbills, have serrated bills that are ideally suited for capturing slippery fish.

At signpost #10 the Yellow, Green, and Blue Trails branch off. If you look straight ahead you'll see the meadow: in summer, a sea of yellow and red grasses punctuated by orange blazes of butterflyweed. We saw each bloom covered with tiny butterflies.

Continuing on the Red Trail you reenter the forest with its stands of tupelo, gray birch, and shadblow. The cherrylike fruit of the shadblow is a food for some of the woodland birds that breed here. But the dominant tree community is oak-hickory, with its attendant understory of viburnum, sassafras, and blueberry. These trees and shrubs, too, provide food for birds. In May, be sure to look for the showy pink flowers of the pinxter azalea. Its Latin name, *Rhododendron nudiflorum,* refers to the fact that the flowers appear before the shrub is fully leafed out. Closer to the forest floor are trailing arbutus and spotted wintergreen—two tiny, but lovely, wildflowers. Arbutus is in the heath family, grows very close to the ground, and has a pale pink (or white) flower, which blooms in early spring (April–May). The wintergreen will bloom from June to August; its flowers are in small clusters at the top of a three- to five-inch stem, nodding, and waxy white or pinkish. Its leaves, near the ground, are dark green, mottled with white.

On the western side of the preserve is a white pine swamp, the only tree and shrub community of its kind on Long Island. It's been designated of "unique local importance" by the state's Department of Environmental Conservation. The swamp is in a glacial kettle, and is characterized by huge mats of sphagnum moss, punctuated by occasional stunted white pines. There is virtually no open water. Organic accumulations are over ten feet thick, and have been dated to 3,900 years. The shrubs include swamp azalea, white alder, buttonbush, and highbush blueberry. A group of taller white pines (twenty-five to forty feet tall) is found in the innermost portion of the swamp. *Usnea,* a species of lichen that grows on saplings and shrubs, is particularly lush here. It's used by ruby-throated hummingbirds in their nests.

Ruby-throated hummingbirds are just one of the eighty-two species of breeding birds at Mashomack. Others include northern bobwhite, piping plover, least tern, belted kingfisher, tree swallow, eastern kingbird, Carolina and house wrens, hermit thrush, northern mockingbird, blue jay, prairie warbler, American redstart, and northern oriole. As you return to the visitors' center, you may see some resident birds at the feeders.

Orient Beach
State Park

Location: Orient
Owner: New York State
Distance: 1–5 miles

A spit extending westward from the mainland into Gardiners Bay, Orient Beach State Park is a product of the movement and accumulation of sand and gravel by tides, currents, and waves over a period of hundreds of thousands of years. Currents carry sand and pebbles from the northeastern tip of Long Island and deposit them at the western end of this peninsula. As it grows westward, it protects Long Beach Bay and Orient Harbor. And in generations to come, Long Beach Bay may well become a lake.

Once called Oysterponds, owing to its bountiful oyster production, the area was settled in the mid-seventeenth century. The sandy peninsula that is now the park was originally called Long Beach, and in the nineteenth century a fish factory was set up here. The remains of this industry are found at the ponds, about 2½ miles from the parking area.

After the fish company went out of business, Long Beach was left idle for about thirty years, becoming both a sanctuary for wildlife and storm protection for the town of Orient. To ensure continued use for these purposes, the land was deeded to the state, and the park was established. One of the stipulations was that the western tip be maintained as a bird sanctuary.

Access

Take the Long Island Expressway to the last exit (#73); continue east on Old Country Road (County Road 58) to NY 25, then NY 25 east to the end. The park is located at the extreme northeastern tip of Long Island. Picnic tables, restrooms, and a restaurant are located adjacent to the parking lot. The restaurant is open from April through Septem-

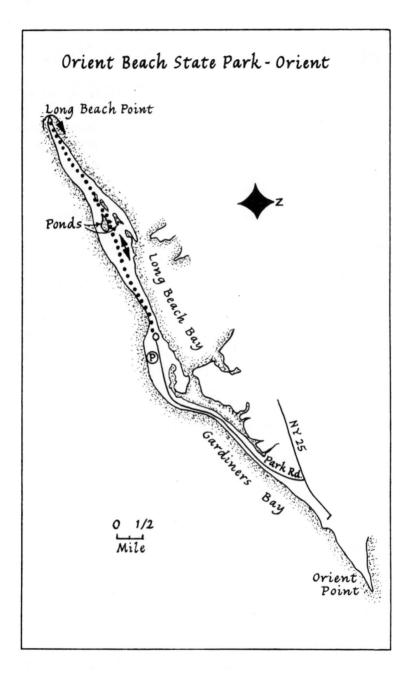

Orient Beach State Park - Orient

ber. The park is open from 8 AM to 8 PM from Memorial Day to Labor Day; the rest of the year the park is open from 8 AM to 4:30 PM. A $4 fee (per car) is charged daily from Memorial Day to Labor Day and on weekends from April 1 to Memorial Day and from Labor Day to Columbus Day.

The park is wheelchair accessible. A special, all-terrain wheelchair is available for use at no charge.

Trail

A track goes down the middle of the spit from the parking lot past freshwater ponds (about 2½ miles) all the way to Long Beach Point (5 miles). Allow the better part of a day to do this 10-mile walk. There was a lighthouse at the point, but in 1963 it was largely destroyed by fire. Volunteer efforts raised enough money to rebuild it, and the beacon now shines again.

While shelling along the beach of Gardiners Bay, you're likely to hear the "kip-kip-kip" call of the osprey as it flies to its nest, often bearing a fish in its talons. Osprey nests are big, untidy masses of sticks and twigs, often placed atop platforms designed for that purpose. The clam, mussel, oyster, scallop, shark-eye, quarter deck, and Atlantic jingle shells that you find are indicative of the richness that lies just beneath the surface.

You might see a jellyfish drifting along, inflating its reddish purple sac, or cap, and swinging out its tentacles as it looks in the shallows for food. A common species here is the lion's mane, also called red jelly, a graceful animal about five inches across, pinkish or yellowish brown, with numerous tentacles. Jellyfish are members of an ancient phylum that includes corals and anemones. Notably sluggish and delicate, jellyfish spend their lives drifting through the water. Zoologist Roger Caras writes, "They sting anything they encounter. They are never in a hurry and have been floating around this way for untold years. It is obviously a successful way of life since billions of them are still around. . . . They just bump and sting, bump and sting."

Along the main track, some areas have been roped off. These are piping plover nest sites. The piping plover is an endangered shorebird, small (5½ inches) and chunky, with a brown back, white underparts, and an incomplete dark band at the neck. The plovers arrive in late March. By April they've established nesting territories. Plovers nest on beaches, and their nests are not much more than scrapes in the sand. The eggs are well camouflaged, too, so it's necessary to protect these sites from people who might accidentally step on a nest. (The chief causes of lost nests are people and their vehicles.) The Nature Conservancy also puts up wire cages around the nests. The purpose of these cages is to protect the eggs and nestlings from foxes.

When the plover chicks hatch (about a month after laying), they are precocial—that is, independent, with open eyes and downy feathers—and can follow their parents and find their own food. We watched a family (an adult with two chicks) out in the track forage for food: insects, marine worms, and crustaceans.

By July the chicks are ready to fly, and both adult and young plovers depart for their wintering grounds (in the Caribbean) in late August and September. The piping plover program at Orient has been quite successful: in 1995 there were eight nests, up from six the year before.

Other shorebirds seen at Orient include American oyster-catcher, snowy egret, ruddy turnstone, and sanderling. Common and least terns dive for fish just off the beach. The least tern is another endangered bird. Least terns also nest in the sand—making a small scrape and laying two or three eggs. Snowfencing is used here, too, to protect the birds and their chicks. Unlike plovers, who try to distract intruders with a "broken-wing" display, terns will dive-bomb you—aiming right for your head. If a tern attacks you, you can be sure you're too close to a nest or chicks. Please move away, quickly and carefully.

As you walk along the track—a few feet higher in elevation than the beach—you'll see many of the expected beach plants: rugosa rose, bayberry, seaside goldenrod, and beach plum. But there are less familiar plants as well: sea lavender, salt wart, and prickly pear. These cactuses, with their cheery yellow flowers, grow close to the ground.

Long Beach Bay

They are the only native cactuses in the Northeast, and grow readily in sandy areas and on open rocky sites. Oaks and eastern redcedar are also native species, but the stands of Japanese black pines were planted by the state. These trees are hardy and durable, and their irregular, wide-open branches allow them to survive in windy places.

If it's not too hot, you might want to walk as far as the ponds. On the way you'll pass by some relics of the old fish factory. The ponds provide fresh water for resident mammals, including deer, fox, raccoons, and rabbits. Birds, too, exploit this resource.

If you visit the park in summer, don't forget to bring your swimsuit. The beaches on both sides are lovely.

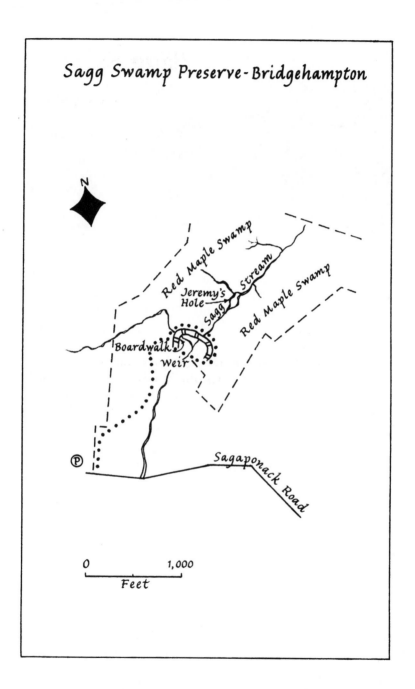

Sagg Swamp Preserve-Bridgehampton

N

Red Maple Swamp

Sagg Stream

Jeremy's Hole

Red Maple Swamp

Boardwalk

Weir

P

Sagaponack Road

0   1,000
      Feet

Sagg Swamp Preserve

Location: Bridgehampton
Owner: The Nature Conservancy
Distance: 1 mile

Sagg Swamp is an oasis of tranquillity that lies only a couple of miles from noisy, crowded Montauk Highway and the bustle of the town of Bridgehampton. A narrow path leads from a back road into a woodland—there's hardly a hint of what's to come.

Left alone for most of the past 300 years—it's only a swamp after all, not worth anything—Sagg is a remnant of a past time. It's a fragment of what was once over much of Long Island: stream and swamp, edged by mixed woodlands. Sagg is a world ruled by water and peat. Cattails poke up through the boards in the boardwalk, eager for sunlight. The sweet, lilylike fragrance of swamp azalea permeates the air. We walk, lulled by the soft mewing of catbirds.

Access

From the town of Southampton, head east on NY 27 (Montauk Highway). Turn right (south) at the stop light in Bridgehampton onto Ocean Road, then turn left (east) on Sagaponack Road. Proceed about 0.7 mile to a Nature Conservancy sign, on the left, just before the small bridge over Sagaponack Pond. Park on the side of the road. The trail begins at the sign. The preserve is open daily during daylight hours. There are no public facilities.

Trail

As soon as you enter the preserve, you're plunged into a mixed woodland, dominated by black oaks. This upland area is quite different from the rest of the preserve. Here, wood anemones and Canada mayflower bloom, while wild rose provides the dense underbrush that catbirds and wrens prefer. You walk on a carpet of brown oak leaves, fallen from the trees last autumn and breaking up now to add a layer of light soil to the forest floor. The waist-high ferns make a hot summer's day seem cool.

As you continue down the narrow path, you'll notice a distinct change, as the red maple takes over. The highbush blueberry and sweet pepperbush of the uplands are still evident as shrubs, but the big trees are now mostly red maple. Sagg is a predominantly red maple swamp, cut through by a freshwater stream. Some of the maples are upturned, blown over by stiff windstorms, because their roots don't reach deep enough into the moist, mossy soil. Cinnamon ferns, royal ferns, spotted touch-me-not (jewelweed), and sphagnum moss all indicate a very moist soil.

At the intersection, turn left. A boardwalk takes you deep into the swamp, crossing duckweed-splotched water that reflects the trees above. Within the swamp are three small Atlantic white cedar groves. White cedar swamps have largely disappeared from Long Island, cut down and drained to make way for "development." Atlantic white cedar (also known as swamp cedar) has a restricted range, mostly along the Atlantic coast. Since the wood is light and strong, the trees used to be in demand for building. Their straight trunks made them popular for utility poles, and although they've been known to grow up to ninety feet in height, most of the ones on Long Island are less than fifty feet tall.

The swamp today provides a home for fourteen species of mammals, including eastern chipmunk, gray squirrel, cottontail rabbit, muskrat, whitetail deer, southern flying squirrel, and mink. The mink is a mustelid—related to otters, weasels, and skunks. About a foot long, minks are a rich, dark brown, with a tiny white chin patch. Their chief foods are crawfish and freshwater minnows. Although raccoons and fox will build dens close to human habitation, minks den along stream or lake banks in more wild areas. According to Stephen Lorence, a wildlife biologist, there are probably more mink now in Suffolk County than at any other time since 1945.

Indian pipe

The 700-foot boardwalk encircles the swamp, giving walkers a rare window onto an otherwise inaccessible world. Cattails, phragmites, and arrowhead grow in big clusters, providing nesting material and food for a variety of birds and other animals. Arrowhead, with its roselike white flowers and arrow-shaped leaves, is easy to identify. Its edible, starchy rhizomes are known as duck potatoes, and are eaten by muskrats and ducks.

The water is rich in vegetation. Leafy pondweeds, watercress, and smartweed are also food for ducks. Mallards and the now endangered American black duck feed here and nest in the margins of the pond. Once among our most common waterfowl, the black duck is suffering from several threats: overhunting, acid rain, and competition from and hybridization with mallards. Since 1980 it has been "blue-listed" by the National Audubon Society.

Downy woodpeckers excavate nesting cavities in the surrounding dead trees, and the impenetrable tangle of vines—greenbrier, Virginia creeper, bittersweet, and poison ivy—provides just the protection small songbirds need. A yellow warbler—like a flying dandelion—darts across the water. "Chirrup-cheeree," calls out the robin. A catbird flies so close that it seems to part your hair. It alights in a rose thicket and cocks its black-capped head, staring at you with its brilliant black eye. The air smells sweet. Swamp azalea, with its white, five-petaled flowers and shiny green leaves, seems to grow everywhere.

As you leave the boardwalk, notice the springiness of the ground beneath your feet—like a trampoline of sphagnum. The trail curves around and there's another, shorter boardwalk, over a weir. You'll then find yourself on the woodland part of the trail. On your way back, keep your eyes open for wildflowers such as Indian pipe, whorled loosestrife, and starflower.

Accabonac Harbor/ Merrill Lake Sanctuary

Location: Springs, East Hampton
Owner: The Nature Conservancy
Distance: 1½ miles

The walk through the meadow and woodlot down to the salt marsh of Accabonac Harbor is like a journey back in time, a return to our primordial origins. The water is the most primitive, giving way to the area of salt marsh cordgrass, which established itself soon after the end of the Wisconsin Ice Age (about 15,000 years ago). The gradual accumulation of organic matter caused the level of the marsh to rise, and salt marsh hay replaced the cordgrass. Early settlers—Bonackers—cut the hay as food for their livestock and also used it as insulation for their houses. The high salt content of the hay was a fire retardant. Farther on, as the marsh becomes drier, beach plum, groundsel bush, marsh elder, and bayberry dominate. These plants are less salt tolerant, and are the beginning of an upland forest—the most "modern" of the plant communities.

Access

From Main Street in East Hampton (NY 27), bear left at the windmill onto North Main Street. Continue under the railroad bridge, past a shopping area, through a traffic light, and bear right at the fork onto Springs Fireplace Road (County Road 41). Proceed 5.5 miles to the preserve sign (on the right). Park on Springs Fireplace Road, and enter the meadow through a turnstile. *When visiting the sanctuary, be sure to close all gates behind you!*

Rubber boots are recommended in all seasons, but are not necessary at low tide. For information about the tides, you can consult the *East Hampton Star* (the local newspaper).

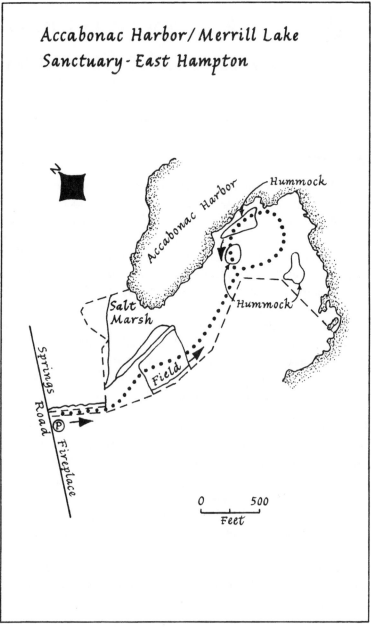

Accabonac Harbor/Merrill Lake Sanctuary - East Hampton

Accabonac Harbor

Hummock

Hummock

Salt Marsh

Field

Springs Road

Fireplace

0   500

Feet

Trail

The trail begins in a meadow, where northern bobwhite are often heard but seldom seen. If you're lucky you might flush a pair. You then continue along the edge of a woodland. This border area, where two habitats meet, is called an ecotone, and ecotones are always good birding spots. Look here for gray catbird (easily told by its "mew" call) and Carolina wren (its call is a loud, repetitive "tea-kettle, tea-kettle, tea-kettle"). Other birds that frequent this area include northern mockingbird, yellow warbler, common yellowthroat, northern oriole, red-winged blackbird, and northern cardinal.

The woodland soon gives way to a bigger meadow, filled with yellow hawkweed, bird's foot trefoil, yarrow, butterflyweed, Deptford pink, and Queen Anne's lace. Here you have your first view of the marsh. Tree and barn swallows glide overhead. An osprey nest (on a platform) is just ahead on the right. Although it doesn't seem like you're really descending, the elevations here are subtle, and even a few inches make a big difference. As you pass through another gate (remember, please, to close it behind you), you're in the marsh itself.

We're standing in the middle of the marsh. Osprey are wheeling above our heads. From where we stand we can see three active nests, each with a pair of youngsters in it. On all sides, salt marsh hay, also known as salt meadow grass *(Spartina patens),* stands about a foot high. But as we look closely we can see other marsh plants: sea lavender, glasswort, and black grass. Sea lavender blooms in July and displays a showy spray of tiny purple flowers. Glasswort, a succulent, resembles a miniature cactus with its jointed, cylindrical stems. In fall it turns bright red.

Suddenly we hear a whistle, "pee-wee-whillet, pee-wee-whillet." A medium-sized brown bird, with bright white wing flashes, flies in circles around us, calling. It's a willet, and we're clearly close to its nest. We move on.

Just ahead is a hummock. These slight mounds support an upland plant community even though they're in the middle of the marsh. Because of their elevation, they're rarely inundated by high tides. A

Drainage ditch cutting through the salt marsh

pair of downy woodpeckers are nesting in a snag. Eastern kingbirds flycatch from an exposed perch. And in a big dead tree is an osprey nest. Be careful of poison ivy, which flourishes in the hummocks.

As you continue on the trail you might see sharp-tailed sparrows dive into the salt marsh cordgrass *(Spartina alterniflora)*. They hop up, then spin down into the grass like whirligigs. Sharp-taileds breed in saltwater marshes, usually raising two broods a season. Their nests are made of a coarse grass and lined with finer grass. The more easily seen song sparrow, with its diagnostic central breast spot, will cling to a stalk out in the open, throw its head back, and sing.

The trail goes around another hummock, close to the shore. Here the path is covered with broken shells: quahogs, mostly, but also scallops, mussels, and periwinkles. At the edge of the high-tide line you can see masses of eelgrass (food for Canada geese) and brown seaweed. A herring gull drifts lazily by. And out on a rock a common tern rests between fishing dives. Straight ahead you can see Louse Point (right) and Cape Gardiner (left). A clean, salty smell pervades the air.

Great egrets—tall, white wading birds—look stately as they stand against the green grass and water. Other birds often seen here include black-crowned night heron, double-crested cormorant, and black skimmer. The skimmer is unique among birds: it's the only species whose lower mandible (the bottom half of its bill) is longer than the upper. This feature enables the bird to "skim" the surface of the water with its bill. When it comes in contact with prey, the bill snaps shut.

The trail loops back and you retrace your steps through the marsh. The drainage ditches that you see were cut in the early 1900s to control mosquitoes, but we prefer to let the swallows and flycatchers take care of them. You'll continue back up through the fields and woodland. The upland areas are the best places to look for the mammals that make the sanctuary their home: raccoon, red fox, and whitetail deer. Various reptiles and amphibians—including eastern hognose and eastern milk snakes and several salamander species—are resident. The best time to find salamanders is in the very early spring.

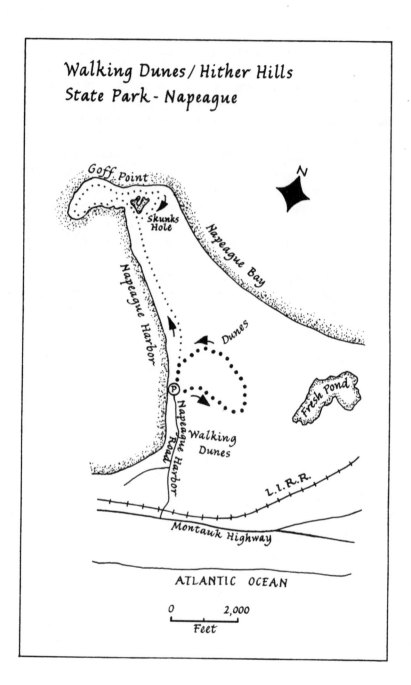

Walking Dunes / Hither Hills
State Park - Napeague

Goff Point

Skunks Hole

Napeague Bay

N

Napeague Harbor

Dunes

Fresh Pond

P

Napeague Harbor Road

Walking Dunes

L.I.R.R.

Montauk Highway

ATLANTIC OCEAN

0   2,000
        Feet

Walking Dunes/ Hither Hills State Park

Location: Hither Hills State Park, Napeague
Owner: New York State and The Nature Conservancy
Distance: about 1 mile

Though Hither Hills State Park is an extensive area, stretching across the south fork from Block Island Sound to the Atlantic Ocean, the small sand spit that reaches out into Napeague Bay is a fascinating spot to visit. At the base of the spit, where it begins its arch around Napeague Harbor, is a trail that passes among the advancing sand dunes to the "phantom forest." Grain by grain, the dunes are flowing (walking) to the southeast, drowning a forest of cherry trees, pitch pine, and mixed oaks, and leaving in their wake a wetland with orchids and other delicate bog plants.

Because of the dynamic nature of this terrain, the trail is sometimes difficult to follow, even obscured. But with a good sense of direction, and suitable footgear for walking in sand, you will have no problem navigating through the woodland and around the dunes to the shore in what is basically a loop trail.

Access

From the eastern edge of Amagansett (the post office), follow NY 27 (Montauk Highway) for 5.3 miles to Napeague Harbor Road. Turn left and take the road to the end. There is limited parking at the trailhead, and without a town sticker, you're liable for a ticket between May 15 and September 15.

Trail

The trail begins directly to the right of the road, and the general idea is to bear left in a circle around the dune. At first you'll pass through a stretch of beach grass punctuated by beach plum shrubs, rugosa

Walking Dunes/Hither Hills State Park

roses, wild cherry saplings, Japanese honeysuckle, and Virginia creeper. The thin, sharp-edged leaves of the beach grass curl in hot weather in an attempt to conserve moisture. But that's just one example of the adaptive energy of this valuable plant. The roots of beach grass clutch the sand and hold it in place, providing a leeward spot where sand grains can amass. In so doing it also ensures a place where the grass can send out new shoots—in fact, the addition of sand to the roots apparently stimulates growth. And since the seaside air is so charged with salt spray, the beach grass leaves have pores through which they take in moisture and expel salt. The wind bends the leaves of this graceful plant downward and they trace a circle in the sand, which is why the plant is sometimes called "compass grass."

In summer, the sprightly pink or white flowers of the rugosa roses are open wide. In fall, the orange rose hips swell to the size of small plums and sometimes are used to make jelly. Though we've become accustomed to seeing the rugosa rose in sandy areas of the United States, it's an introduced species from Japan.

Very soon you enter a shrubby forest, mainly oaks, with bayberry scattered about and some bearberry—an evergreen creeping vine with bell-like white flowers and large red berries—at your feet. In May and June, Canada mayflower and white starflower can be seen blooming. At the fork, continue straight ahead through a hollow (called a blowout, where strong winds have carved a gap in the dunes), and at the next fork, turn right and continue around the dune, keeping it on the left. Scarlet and black oaks and pitch pine predominate in this sheltered area behind the dune. How quiet it is, except for the gentle rustle of the stiff brown oak leaves that remain on the trees from last year.

The area behind the dune is called a swale. The vegetation grows here, not so much because it is protected from fierce sea breezes or the soil is richer; it is not, necessarily. A refuge of fresh air, the swale is created when the salt air blows over the dunes and is sent upward— similar to the way air flow is directed over a plane's wing to create lift. Plants that cannot tolerate salt are able to grow in a swale. Note: In this part of the trail, the path is not clearly marked, but that's not important; just follow the dune, keeping it on the left. Where there's a clearing, turn left and walk along the dune, partway down from the ridge. The path will lead you up and over the dune.

If you look at a sand dune from a little distance, you'll see that it is shaped like an airfoil, a long, smooth, rising slope on the side facing the prevailing winds. Most dunes travel landward; drifting sand is piled up and blown over the crest, then gravity brings it to rest at its natural angle of repose, about 30 degrees, on the leeward side of the ridge. These dunes at Napeague are walking, for sure. It is believed that timber harvesting and roads built in the area years ago destabilized the land and left it vulnerable. At the top of the ridge, you can see how far the dunes have advanced and where they are headed. Some stabilization attempts have been made, but migrating dunes are a natural phenomenon that's not easily halted.

At the summit, you'll get a marvelous view of Napeague Harbor and be able to see the spit to its tip, Goff Point. Beyond is Block Island Sound, with Gardiners Island on the horizon. Trace the curves of some of the smaller dunes below for a bird's-eye look at how the northwest winds form horseshoe shapes from the blowing sand. Where the sand is darker, the heavier garnet and magnetite particles have remained while the lighter quartz grains have moved on.

Descend into the bowl; this is the phantom forest—the devastation that follows the passage of the dunes. At this point, there aren't any remnants of trees left—after all, dunes do travel slowly—but smaller vegetation has been colonizing this area. Directly ahead is a cranberry bog; you'll want to walk to the left of this area because rose pogonia and grass pink, two species of orchid, grow here.

As you walk back toward the beach, note the fuchsia flowers of the beach pea, a vine that grows where the dunes are well established. At the tide line is what Philip Kopper, in his book *The Wild Edge,* calls "tidal litter": pieces of eelgrass, seaweeds, bits of shell, and the occasional plastic discards.

You can walk to Goff Point from here; just pick up the sand road on the right, which will take you through a meadow of beardgrass and switchgrass, and then in a loop around Skunks Hole—a small pond near the tip. You'll return the same way.

The road and parking area are about fifty feet to the left, along the beach.

Montauk Point State Park

Location: Montauk
Owner: New York State
Distance: 1–2 miles

This is land's end. And wind is the theme here. Though invisible, it affects all life at the point. Plants and songbirds seek shelter from the wind, while out at sea the wind roils the water, bringing food to the wintering seabirds. The horizon is all around you. You're close to the elements. The wind rustles the grasses, turned yellow, the color of straw. Waves crash on the shore; gulls cry as they sail overhead, borne by the wind.

Access

From the town of Montauk, drive 5.5 miles east to the end of NY 27. Public restrooms and picnic tables are located by the parking lot. A restaurant, with public restrooms and a small gift shop, is across the road.

The lighthouse and museum are open daily from June 1 to October 30, 10:30 AM to 6 PM; weekends only from November 1 to May 31, 10:30 AM to 4:30 PM. Holiday weekends have different hours; for information, call 516-668-2544. The lighthouse is operated by the Montauk Historical Society, and tours are given every hour from 11:30; the cost is $2.50.

Park admission is $4 per car (daily in summer and weekends year-round).

Trail

There is no established trail; you just walk along the shoreline. As you leave the restaurant, head downhill toward the beach. If you turn right you'll go toward the point and around the lighthouse. In winter

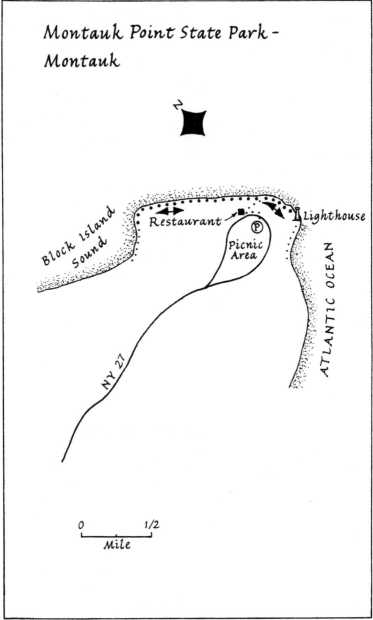

Montauk Point State Park –
Montauk

Block Island Sound

Restaurant

Picnic Area

Lighthouse

ATLANTIC OCEAN

NY 27

0   1/2
Mile

this is the best place for birds, although the overlook just behind the restaurant is also a good vantage point.

Rafts of red-breasted mergansers, common eider, and white-winged and surf scoters congregate at the point. Occasionally razorbill, king eider, harlequin duck, and black scoter can also be seen. Both red-throated and common loons are present in good numbers, and northern gannets dive from the sky like fighter planes. Black-legged kittiwakes (small gulls) are often among the winter visitors.

The rough water here churns up lots of food for these seabirds, which breed much farther north, in places like Baffin Bay. Although a spotting scope is useful (but not if it's windy), the loons will often come in quite close. Since both loons are in winter plumage, the best way to tell them apart is to look at their bills. The red-throated's slender bill is upturned, and the bird has a slimmer appearance overall than that of the common loon. Scoters, too, are easy to distinguish: the black is all black; the white-winged is black with white on the wings; and the surf has white on the head and a multicolored bill. Long-tailed duck (formerly called oldsquaw) is also a frequent winter visitor. In winter it looks very white, its long, upward-pointing tail being its best field mark.

We've had harlequin ducks—the prettiest of all seabirds, we think—come in so close we didn't need binoculars. These small, colorful ducks are uncommon, but every couple of years they're seen. They, too, breed in the far north, and winter in heavy surf along rocky coasts from Maine to New Jersey. They're bluish gray, with a large reddish flank, and bold white stripes on breast and back. Their heads, too, are patterned with red and white.

Among the most unusual sightings is sure to be the razorbill. A relative of the now extinct great auk, razorbills are alcids, not ducks. This family of seabirds swim underwater, using their wings to propel them; they come ashore only to breed. Razorbills are white below and black above, with a thin white ring around their thick bills. They're usually found farther from shore than the ducks.

If you turn around (or left as you leave the restaurant) and head west-northwest for about a mile, you'll come to the best place to see seals. Their shiny heads bobbing up and down in the water look like

Montauk lighthouse

boulders. These are mostly harbor seals, but the occasional harp and gray are sometimes also seen. The harbor seal has a heavily spotted back, whereas the harp seal is pale gray to yellow on the back with a dark band. The gray seal also has a spotted back, but is much larger and has a more deliberate manner than the harbor seal. Winter, too, is the best time to see the harbor seals, because most of them leave for their Canadian breeding grounds by mid-April. (A few stay year-round in Peconic Bay.)

Along the beach, gulls—herring and great black-backed—drop their catch on the rocks to smash the shells, leaving just the broken bits of crabs and other crustaceans. Near the cliff, the damp sand smells faintly fishy. The seaweed drapes itself on rocks at the water's edge. When the waves touch shore and retreat, the seaweed sways like a hula dancer.

The thickets just in from the beach, protected as they are, are good for spotting wintering songbirds, as are the trees by the parking lot. Swamp sparrows, told by their rusty crowns and white throats; white-throated sparrows, distinguished by their white throats and black-and-white striped heads; black-capped chickadees; tufted titmice; and northern mockingbirds are all resident. Occasionally pine siskins or common redpolls will make an appearance. Siskins are small, brownish finches with yellow wing bars and yellow at the base of the tail. They are irregularly common in large flocks, and prefer conifers. In many ways they resemble goldfinches, with which they sometimes flock. Redpolls are a little bigger (5 inches) and are also brownish on the back but have a bright red cap, black chin, and reddish throat. They, too, are irregular, but do wander down from the north in large flocks. Be sure not to confuse them with either house finches (common year-round residents) or purple finches (also a winter visitor). Both finches are larger and much redder overall.

We love Montauk in the winter when it's at its best. Though people may find it harsh and rugged, it is a great sanctuary for wildlife, which finds much-needed food and shelter here.

Selected Reading

As we suggest in our preface, it's always good to have a few field guides along. We've found the Peterson series *(Birds, Reptiles and Amphibians, Mammals, Ferns,* and *Wildflowers)* to be particularly useful. In addition, we can recommend the following:

Anderson, Scott Edward. *Walks in Nature's Empire.* Woodstock, Vt.: The Countryman Press, Inc., 1995.

Brockman, C. Frank. *Trees of North America.* New York: Golden Press, 1968.

Glassberg, Jeffrey. *Butterflies Through Binoculars: A Field Guide to Butterflies in the Boston–New York–Washington Region.* New York: Oxford University Press, 1993.

Milne, Lorus and Margery. *The Audubon Society Field Guide to Insects and Spiders.* New York: Alfred A. Knopf, 1980.

Niering, William A., and Nancy Olmstead. *The Audubon Society Field Guide to North American Wildflowers; Eastern Region.* New York: Alfred A. Knopf, 1979.

Turner, John L. *Exploring the Other Island: A Seasonal Guide to Nature on Long Island.* Great Falls, Va.: Waterline Books, 1994.

Environmental Organizations

Although there are many national organizations that support nature conservation, these are some local chapters and groups.

The Nature Conservancy
Long Island Chapter
250 Lawrence Hill Road
Cold Spring Harbor, NY 11724
516-367-3225

Sierra Club/Long Island
PO Box 210
Syosset, NY 11791-0210

New York City Butterfly Club
Don Riepe, Secretary
29 West Ninth Road
Broad Channel, NY 11693

Group for the South Fork
PO Box 569
Bridgehampton, NY 11932
516-537-1400

Long Island Pine Barrens Society
PO Box 429
Manorville, NY 11949
516-369-3300

Huntington Audubon Society
PO Box 735
Huntington, NY 11743

South Shore Audubon Society
PO Box 31
Freeport, NY 11520

Lyman Langdon Audubon Society
PO Box 763
Port Washington, NY 11050

Moriches Bay Audubon Society
PO Box 802
Center Moriches, NY 11934

Four Harbors Audubon Society
Box 126
East Setauket, NY 11733

Greenbelt Trail Conference
23 Deer Path Road
Central Islip, NY 11722-3403
516-360-0753

Index